THE INEQUALITY ADVANTAGE
THE PRINCIPLES OF COVERT POWER

THE INEQUALITY ADVANTAGE

PRINCIPLES OF COVERT POWER

THE INEQUALITY ADVANTAGE

Published by Mitch Vandell Publishing
www.MitchVandell.com

First Printing: 2015

www.theInequalityAdvantage.com
www.BargepoleManagement.com

Printed and bound by Mitch Vandell Publishing.
Layout by: Yosef Alemayehu
For purchase orders email info@MitchVandell.com

ISBN: 978-1514756430

PRINCIPLES OF COVERT POWER

THE INEQUALITY ADVANTAGE

The secret of life is to appreciate the pleasure of being terribly, terribly deceived.
—Oscar Wilde

TABLE OF CONTENTS

PREFACE

BOOK II:
THE BARGEPOLE COEFFICIENT -
OPTIMIZING CONTROL AND UTILITY OF PERSONNEL

INTRODUCTION:
IMPACT OF BARGEPOLE MANAGEMENT THEORY ON ORGANIZATIONS
CHAPTER 1: THE ORGANIZATIONAL BENEFITS OF BARGEPOLE MANAGEMENT
CHAPTER 2: DANGERS AND PITFALLS TO ORGANIZATIONS

BOOK III: BLISSFULLY EXPLOITED
PROMOTING SOCIAL TOLERANCE TO BENEFIT FROM THE PUBLIC'S SELF-
OPPRESSION
CHAPTER 1: GLOBAL HIERARCHICAL INTERDEPENDENCE
CHAPTER 2: NATION-BUILDING

BONUS MATERIAL: BARGEPOLE MANAGEMENT
PREFACE: YOU TOO CAN BECOME A BARGEPOLE MANAGER!
AUTHOR'S NOTE
INTRODUCTION TO AND OVERVIEW OF BARGEPOLE MANAGEMENT

BOOK I: CREATING YOUR UNFAIR ADVANTAGE
CHAPTER 1: LEARNING FROM THE MASTERS
CHAPTER 2: THE SELF-ACCEPT PSYCHOLOGY
CHAPTER 3: THE ECONOMIC PRINCIPLES OF BARGEPOLE THEORY
CHAPTER 4: A HOW-TO GUIDE: IMPLEMENTING THE BARGEPOLE STRATEGY

APPENDIX: THE PSYCHOLOGY OF COUNTER-POSITIVE THINKING

THE INEQUALITY ADVANTAGE

PREFACE

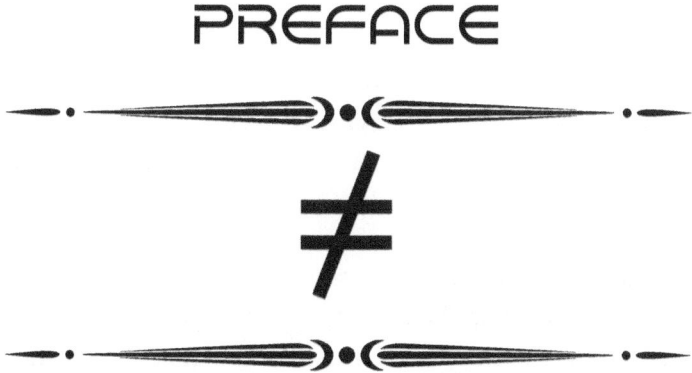

The most dominant and technically advanced civilizations throughout history have all prospered by creating massive divides between a ruling elite and masses of workers. These power differentials between groups have maximized productivity and cost efficiency. They have allowed a concentrated clique at the top to reap the lion's share of rewards. This principle has been seen in ancient Egypt to the Roman and British Empires. Access to extremely cheap, controllable, and interchangeable labor is as critical to the success of corporations and nations today as it was in earlier eras. As will be shown in this book, modern day capitalist societies led by American-styled corporatism have evolved with more refined and sophisticated methods for securing workers at minimal cost. From physically forcing chosen groups to work without pay, the system has evolved into workers being voluntarily exploited.

Contrary to popular opinion, slavery was not as economically beneficial to the United States as many presume. In an excerpt from his book, America: Imagine a World Without Her, Dinesh D'Souza makes the following comment: "Slavery provides no incentive for slaves to work, since they don't get to keep the product of their labor. But neither does slavery encourage masters to work, because slaves do the work for them. Remarkably, slavery is bad for masters and slaves: it degrades work, so less work is done." D'Souza refers to Alexis de Tocqueville, who travelled extensively across America in the early nineteenth century and reflected on the contrast between the "industrious Ohio," which was prospering, with the "idle Kentucky," which was dilapidated by comparison. With climate and conditions being very similar, de Tocqueville's conclusion was that the disparity was attributable to the practice of slavery in the latter

America is likely to never have risen to dominance if the Confederate States had won the Civil War. However, the slave culture mentality that restrained the American people was in time replaced by the so-called Bargepole Superstructure. As will be explained in the chapters ahead, this is a far superior recipe for securing cost-effective and submissive labor. False meritocracies incentivize workers and uphold their naive belief that effort and skill are commensurately rewarded. Concurrently, the outsized rewards that only a handful of people enjoy are presented as both fair and very possibly within the same reach of the masses and general population.

The book 'Bargepole Management: The Art of Getting Priced at a Premium' introduced a theory for individuals to benefit over colleagues within an organization. The theory views individual employees as separate economic agents. Each acts in a market that is represented by the organization where traditional market theories apply. This perspective aims to demonstrate how a person can benefit from pursuing a more raw and direct self-interest. How individuals create and uphold inequalities to benefit them is primarily the skill of cultivating an image of being critical for results while making decisions, input and contribution impossible to identify, trace or measure. The tools for achieving this involve social psychology and the ability to influence organizational structure and communication.

The book you are holding now, The Inequality Advantage, expands onto the collective and society at large. The aim is to show how the same Bargepole Management philosophies can be scaled and applied across groups in decentralized yet predictable patterns. The approach is presented as a framework for inspiring behaviors that encourage groups in organizations and in society to voluntarily act against their self-interests for the benefit of others

Modern-day examples include outsourcing manufacturing to sweatshops in China or bonded laborers imported from the Indian subcontinent to work in extreme heat on construction sites around the world. In the West, illegal aliens without civil rights keep US farming and agricultural activities profitable by accepting work conditions and pay that Americans simply won't tolerate. Likewise, in urban cities, legions of skilled professionals accept city office jobs with extreme working hours and almost no pay.

The main enabler is the ability to create power distances between groups to make objective discussions of fairness easier to avoid. This makes disparate interests of different groups possible to present as congruent and as sharing the same aims and objectives. Despite certain groups being heavily favored at the expense of others an increased social stability is established along with greater productivity that benefits everyone.

Expanding from the perspective of the individual to a broader context, the first part of this book looks at how bargepoling impacts organizations both as a potential competitive advantage as well as a liability. The second and final part explores how the same methods of bargepoling apply in societies at large to fuel economic activity.

The motive with this book is not to argue or push any political ideology, defend exploitation or make accusations against any specific group I see as benefiting at the expense of others. Rather, I hope to encourage your self-evaluation and introspection to challenge and expand your worldview by getting you to question the following:

- ▶ To what degree are we aware of choosing lifestyle habits that are self-sabotaging in that they limit our potential and prospects while being to the benefit of others?
- ▶ Why are people encouraged to reject the idea of distinguishable features defining and separating social groups?
- ▶ Can shared interests be represented and pursued if they can't be recognized?

These questions lead up to the most important question that lay hidden in plain sight: who stands to gain by weakening social norms and discipline to thereby create a global population relegated to becoming one single, large, indistinguishable, and powerless mass?

Seeing how the framework of Bargepole Theory applies in society reveals whose interests are being served and how. I hope that after reading this book you will recognize how important and central these questions are in shaping power structures today.

OVERVIEW OF BARGEPOLE MANAGEMENT THEORY

The main tenets of Bargepole Management Theory are based around building a hierarchy with limited transparency for the purpose of influencing communication between layers of an organization so to present yourself as favorably and valuable as possible. A line-up of firewalls insulates from operational accountability and interaction with the frontline staff of so called jimpees (useful idiot workers).

The jimpees are the lifeblood of an organization and they naïvely buy into vague promises of being rewarded in an unspecified future. Central to this approach is establishing a false meritocracy to perpetuate the illusion that rewards are distributed fairly and according to the value of skill and contribution.

Whether bargepoling as a management approach is a benefit or a liability to an organization depends on how it is practiced. The model works when the number of bargepolers is limited and when they are consciously aware of their limitations in knowledge and expertise. Crucially, capable jimpees and firewalls are able to function autonomously and without interference. However, the model is easily unbalanced by an excessive number of bargepolers burdening an organization. At worst, they fail to realize their lack of relevancy in areas of competence and, therefore, involuntarily sabotage operations with their input.

Where an organization is on this spectrum determines its bargepole coefficient. This is intended figuratively and is not a precise number. Maximizing results from positive bargepole behaviors entails a positive coefficient. The opposite, a negative coefficient, is when bargepole behaviors become counter-productive. In such cases, the common euphemism used is "lack of leadership." What it is really about is a surplus of counter-productive leadership.

While this may be plain for anyone to see, stating this reality and suggesting improvements is difficult. There are rarely any benefits for anyone to do so. The consequences impact individual employees that are denied meaningful work environments while restraining the overall competitiveness of organizations.

Exploring why, how and when these behaviors occur, making them recognizable and understanding their influence on organizations, is the subject of this second installment of this series. The aim is to create a discussion about these behaviours that are widely recognized yet rarely addressed openly. Why are they so common and difficult to avoid? Why do they take root in organizations? What are the potential benefits and liabilities to employees and organizations alike? What are the best ways to adapt or counter-act these realities?

BOOK II

THE BARGEPOLE COEFFCIENT

—

OPTIMIZING CONTROL AND UTILITY OF PERSONNEL

THE INEQUALITY ADVANTAGE

INTRODUCTION

IMPACT OF BARGEPOLE MANAGEMENT
THEORY ON ORGANIZATIONS

Few organizations set out or aim to promote styles of bargepole management. Instead, the organization tends to become prone to bargepoling as a consequence of the individuals who claw themselves into senior positions, become stuck, and then start protecting each other's backs. Alternatively, bargepoling is often a means to an end for the individuals in an organization to respond to the practical needs of the business model. For instance, if a company's business model is to rip off customers by misrepresenting the product or service, those people responsible for this deceit need a way to rationalize their own behavior.

Examples of these schemes are unscrupulous telesales that flog financial services, credit cards from banks, useless insurance policies, self-help seminars, get-rich-quick schemes of multi-level marketing, and over-promised benefits for participating in an exhibition or at a conference. Another instance occurs when the means of manufacturing is immoral. Examples include when workers in a third-world countries are treated unfairly or are held to work under inhumane conditions.

The first chapter of this book will look at how bargepoling can be of benefit to the interests of an organization as a whole.

CHAPTER I

THE ORGANIZATIONAL BENEFITS OF BARGEPOLE MANAGEMENT

Ideal market conditions and fine-tuned bargepoling can enable an organization to maximize utility of resources by creating power differentials between hierarchical layers. This maximization is possible through optimal categorization and allocation of workers by avoiding emotional considerations as to fairness of compensation and work conditions between groups. Thereby, a strong competitive advantage is offered.

A central facet is how power differentials are deliberately created between members in organizations to leverage the leeway for more decisive and direct operational action; these power differentials are created by leaders' impunity to not have to justify the reasons for blatant unfairness between groups and individuals. Moreover, these principles of bargepole management are ancient, going back to the dawn of human civilization. As noted in the first book, the British perfected the principles of bargepole management with their colonies. The organizational stability it achieved effectively avoided the risks of confrontation by removing direct comparisons between groups.

CONFLICT AVOIDANCE THROUGH GROUP FRAGMENTATION

Collaboration is difficult, even in culturally homogenous groups, and in culturally diverse expat environments, it is even more complicated. Yet, as argued previously by using the example of India as a British colony, these environments offer optimal conditions for maximizing yield from manpower by applying bargepole management. Again, this situation is due to the flexibility in what is seen as an acceptable treatment by restricting the flow of information and limiting what topics get seen as acceptable to address and discuss.

Paradoxically, ethnically diverse environments do not encourage understanding, acceptance, or tolerance between groups through increased interaction and exchange of ideas. No, the opposite is, in fact, seen as being ordinary. Groups that self-segregate don't compare or relate to each other easily. As a consequence, roles and tasks can more easily be delegated according to group belonging, and the how or why of inequalities can go unquestioned.

The value of having clear structure, focus, and theme in a collaborative environment becomes amplified when effective categorization and control of resources is possible. Highly diverse environments, consisting of groups with little interconnection, allow for better stratification to allocate function according to utility. An example of a micro-cosmos that demonstrates how perfectly this approach can work is the staff on a luxury cruise ship. Even in a closed and limited space, the staff instinctively and voluntarily sections themselves off according to the group affiliation they define and are able to work together with well-structured and harmonious circumstances.

Leadership and management is rarely about having the skill to identify what resources and actions are required to achieve a certain outcome. Instead, the challenges lie in getting access to those resources and in having the necessary measures to ensure that the work is completed. The ability to overcome both of these challenges will dramatically change what is possible to deliver.

Consider the greatest collaborative achievements of any historical civilization. From Machu Picchu to the pyramids in Egypt to the Great Wall of China, such projects were possible because of extreme power differentials between workers and their masters. The greater the concern for fairness, the more restricted laborers' capacity appears to be.

The enabling element in highly diverse expat environments is that the definition of normal and acceptable is unclear. This lack of clarity is not due to how things are discussed, but instead, is caused by what those in a position of power are able to keep out of the discussion completely. Fragmented social groupings further inhibit shared norms to form and take root.

As a hypothetical experiment, consider the following implausible scenario taking place in the United States today. Tens of thousands of construction workers are legally imported from the Indian sub-continent to live in labor camps under strict control at a microscopic fraction of the living standards, work conditions and salaries expected and granted to the local population. For this to take place in a sanctioned and organized manner in the US today is unthinkable. Yet, this is what takes place across much of Asia and the Middle East where vast numbers of foreign people accept work forms that are unacceptable to their local populations. This practice is conducted with efficiency under clear rules and guidelines with little objection from the workers or the states of their home countries. For instance, in Arab countries like Lebanon, Libya, Iran and Iraq with populations considered poor by Western standards, middle class families importing a live-in maid from countries in Africa or the Indian Sub-continent is not uncommon. At the same time, the idea of a citizen taking such a job in his or her own country is unthinkable, despite massive unemployment among the locals in

Large cities with high diversity and expat environments are particularly conducive to practice inequalities such as these. The lack of a common framework of norms in which to compare is ideal for leveraging the benefits of institutionalized inequalities and power differentials. Since the majority of the workers are guests, the tolerance levels for reasonable working demands are increased. If for no other reason than to set benchmarks or comparisons, these tolerance levels are established as the norm.

Consider how deriving the same productivity and control of workers as what is achieved in the Gulf would be impossible to do in the workers' home countries like India, Pakistan and Bangladesh. In the meantime, the same can be said for illegal immigrants arriving to the US from Mexico and Central America. The value from their work efforts is significantly higher than what is achievable to derive from the same workers had they been employed in their home countries. This is for the exact same reasons as described above as applying to guest workers in the Gulf.

ACHIEVING OPTIMAL LABOR UTILIZATION

Bargepole Management and its use of artificial and deliberate creation of large power differences in organizational hierarchies means that increased leverage and leeway can be taken for more decisive and direct action. The ability to practice bargepoling appears to be in direct proportion to an organization's absence of shared social identity (i.e., degree of diversity). In turn, this lack of shared social identity determines the degree to which bargepoling is necessary for maintaining organizational stability as a means of minimizing risk of conflict.

This Bargepole Management strategy of maximizing distances and fragmenting groups can be seen around the world from Libya, the Middle East and to the US, where migrant laborers work under very different rules and conditions than what is applied to its citizens. Moreover, this strategy is one of the more unexplored, or rather, non-contested, areas of management theory about how to minimize friction and conflict in organizations.

How this bargepole strategy is applied today is seen in how promoting the benefits of diversity and integration in name counter-intuitively restrains wider interaction and social mobility of a population in practice. Governance is therefore about convincingly projecting legitimacy of power differentials and inequalities between groups by hiding them in plain sight. Otherwise, discontent and demoralization can spread quickly; this situation can happen by simply allowing the merit of positions and hierarchies to be objectively questioned. When such questioning occurs, diversity becomes a risk and a liability.

The weakening of social cohesion between groups of employees (or jimpees) inhibits the formation of shared norms and mutual interests. The power that a bargepoler commands from controlling communication is compromised when jimpees share and compare information about the organization. The bargepoler's power is further compromised when the jimpees proclaim unfairness about the bargepoler receiving rewards without being of any real use.

Bargepole Management Theory offers a psychological edge that essentially works by influencing and controlling perceptions as well as flows of information in an organization.

The tools available in Bargepole Management Theory to take conscious and deliberate action to influence both perceptions and behaviors are primarily one of the following two types of skills:

▶ Interpersonal social manipulation skills with non-communication, non-committal, and above-reproach skills in avoiding certain topics and questions in discussion

- ▶ Social engineering skills that impact practical aspects of the work environment with composition of staff, flows of information, and power differentials between layers in a hierarchy.

When executing both these types of skillsets together in a concerted effort, it is possible to control flows of information and social behaviors to thereby maximize the utilization of jimpees.

The social engineering element is most typically found in the objective of maintaining a high staff turnover. A bargepoler tries to maintain a high staff turnover in order to avoid exposing his or her lack of competence and overall minimal value to the organization. This anonymity of sorts is possible by restraining staff from gathering and sharing observations about how the bargepoler operates within the organization. Furthermore, when the jimpee staff is in a state of constant flux, loyalties are deterred from being developed that could possibly turn into a liability.

The manipulation skills are mainly used to obstruct the flow of communication by minimizing interaction and inter-communication between jimpee staff members. A silent office is maintained, and communication is obscured between layers of the hierarchy.

Obscuring communication is particularly prevalent among banks and companies active in financial services. Specifically, these organizations obscure information when they take on a higher risk exposure than what clients have accepted or that push the boundaries of being legally compliant. Classic Bargepole Theory enables the bargepolers in a bank, caught up in illegal trading activity, to claim blissful ignorance. The people taking the fall will be the firewalls and the jimpees.

In order for any bargepoler to get away with claiming this blissful ignorance, a fully intact bargepole organization structure is required—one with airtight barriers for communication between layers. Moreover, the bargepoler must possess perfect skills of Management by Non-Communication. These skills involve actively discouraging discussion, compartmentalizing, or making information unavailable, and not offering clarifications as to who knows what or who is responsible for various aspects of an operation.

When executed correctly, Management by Non-Communication will ensure that decisions and accountability are obscured by the lack of transparency in communication within the four main hierarchy layers. No one is exactly clear on who is ultimately responsible in the diffused operational power structure. The bargepoler simply never makes any definite calls or acknowledges accountability for anything, and no one knows what he or she has actually sanctioned, if anything.

Many companies institutionalize Bargepole Theory into their business models either deliberately or by default. This institutionalization occurs when divides are created between individual employees, separating their accountability from that of the company and its managers. Corporations that deliberately remain unaware of the work conditions and environmental record of companies they outsource work to are following basic bargepole procedure. The same goes for the endless examples of how companies that hide behind walls of customer service representatives who have no authority or ability to do anything besides reading the script they have in front of them.

THE INEQUALITY ADVANTAGE

CHAPTER 2

DANGERS AND PITFALLS TO ORGANIZATIONS

GROUP THINK AND DEMORALIZED STAFF

A symptom among organizations where extreme bargepole traits can be observed is their tendency to develop major blind spots to their own conditions. These organizations often display similar traits to those of any cult. In this way, the leaders have brainwashed the organization's members with delusions that are impacting their abilities to correctly interpret realities in the marketplace.

When significant shifts occur in the marketplace, bargepole organizations are likely the least capable to deal with such changes. The senior management takes on a bunker mentality and encourages a cult-like following where the employees start buying into the delusions of their senior management or otherwise get shunned. It even becomes difficult for employees to discuss critical operational issues or address fundamentally flawed business plans with senior management.

Examples where these tendencies can be observed are among many industry giants. The music industry bigwigs doggedly refused to consider alternative modes of online music delivery that did not involve CDs. Nokia and Blackberry, who both held leading positions in the mobile device industry, now, in relative terms when compared to competitors such as Apple, Samsung, and Google, cease to exist as a consequence of refusing to recognize the shift to touch screen smart phones in a timely manner. Other examples include American car manufacturers and major airlines going bankrupt in part from failing to adapt, modernize, or improve their market offerings as a response to customer demand.

There are many dangers in taking bargepoling too far. Whenever painfully obvious or embarrassing mistakes are uncovered in large corporations, managers in senior positions, who presumably have the job of knowing what is going on, are often staggeringly unaware or can't remember anything. Such occurrences are often unmistakable signs of a bargepole organization.

In essence, bargepoling is about separating oneself from objective comparison. Success in this principle can result in the positive outcome of being "priced at a premium." Simultaneously, you must be aware of the dangers involved with adopting a twisted view of yourself, the organization, and the overall environment in which you operate.

The seed of most of the systemic failure in companies is when the self-interest of individuals is misaligned with that of the organization as a whole. Then, when organizations grow with too many bargepolers attached, these individuals are exceedingly concerned about key performance indicators and cost-savings at the expense of delivering actual value to the customer. The personal goal of internally being perceived as more successful than fellow divisional managers becomes more important than wanting to see the company outperform its competitors in the market.

When bargepolers dominate an organization with an unwillingness to assume responsibility for a problem or dedicate the needed financial resources in which to develop a solution, it is a sign that bargepoling may have gone too far. In such environments, even associating yourself with a problem by simply identifying it can potentially cost you your job.

AVOIDING MISALIGNED INCENTIVES

The greatest risks are never the ones you can see, measure, or plan responses to; instead, the greatest risks are most often what you can't see and can never measure. So why the temptation to narrowly predefine what results to use to evaluate success? In a way, that is difficult to foresee; this can create incentives that are misaligned and prove detrimental to the overall outcome. As some say, you can't manage what you can't measure. If that is what you assume, you'd better be darn sure that what you are measuring is what you are trying to manage.

Key Performance Indicators (or KPIs) are intended for basing broad generalizations when sweeping decisions are needed. Nevertheless, the best KPIs are those that are not revealed to employees and thereby do not risk diverting focus from more-important priorities. The best KPIs are designed by identifying what an employee achieves at the peak of his or her potential when doing the job as they are supposed to.

When the KPIs of what a good job is are defined to the employee at the start, conflicting KPIs are easily put in place, with the consequence of promoting counterproductive behaviors and insular thinking. Not least, employees with self-respect find it demoralizing for others to assume they do not understand what needs to be done, are not working hard enough to meet expectations, or are simply not good enough to do so.

An example of such a situation in practice was described in a Vanity Fair feature story about Steve Ballmer. The former CEO of Microsoft used KPIs to consistently identify the weakest performing employees in order to have them fired. The result was a tech company that was practically stripped of the ability to achieve any significant innovation. The staff was not motivated to support each other, because in doing so, they might benefit the KPI of another colleague and, thus, risk losing their job. A related scenario, where the presence of KPIs in an organization was to its detriment, is when the only way to keep your job is to present unrealistic sales targets and thereafter find a way to not be held accountable when they are missed. In one case I knew, a division had four sales directors who would argue about strategy and forecasts while only two sales executives were involved in any actual sales activities. While they would sit in an open office landscape, most communication would be via e-mail. When the forecasts were missed, the two sales executives would be blamed, fired, and replaced, and the cycle would begin again. About once a year, the least senior of the sales directors would also get the boot. Though the lunacy of this is plain for anyone to see, the only real question was: If you are so smart, why aren't you one of those bargepolers?

Organizations with this kind of excessive bargepoling often see the same behaviors in all levels of employees:

1.   They oversell.

2.   They under deliver.

3.   They find excuses.

What is important to realize with these examples and how they relate to Bargepole Management is that KPIs do not exist only for the purpose of improving the performance or results of an organization. KPIs are in place primarily to justify the existence of the bargepole managers, to give the appearance of active decision-making that appears carefully considered, with a scientific approach.

Despite being superfluous, if not outright counterproductive, bargepole managers are able to survive based merely on being good enough at following general trends. The important consideration is that for KPIs to be an effective tool in bargepoling, they must be designed so as not to demoralize and to keep jimpees from working their best and hardest. The carrot must be dangled so it always feels like it's within reach!

As a management approach, bargepole management theory is a double-edged sword. If the balance is off, it tends to become a burden and a handicap quickly, making companies irrelevant. History is packed with such examples, particularly of companies that stagnate in competitiveness and innovation.

INNOVATIVE DIS-ECONOMIES OF SCALE

When companies grow beyond a certain size, their capability to innovate is at risk of declining. As a result, bargepole organizations must be effectively managed so as to allow ideas to be developed autonomously instead of the organization itself being an obstruction. Otherwise, bargepole organizations can fall victim to engaging in initiatives and routines either unrelated to or that directly impede their supposed end goal and purpose.

Increasing the wellbeing of both our lives and businesses depends on innovation that can solve actual needs and increase efficiencies. This is separate from innovation as a gimmick to fuel commerce and to be able to charge a premium. Real innovation is about finding the inflection point of the greatest possible utility at the highest possible simplicity. Herein lies the relationship between seemingly disparate works of genius, such as Beethoven's Ninth, the T-Ford, or the iPhone.

Today, the term innovation is used so much that it has practically become a meaningless buzzword. At the same time, innovation is billed as the Holy Grail for overcoming every modern challenge. Therefore, what does innovation truly mean if it is to be beneficial for a company or organization? Failing to answer this question can make the very pursuit of innovation in and of itself lead to failure.

As expressed by Einstein, innovation is ideally about aiming for the goal of "as simple as possible, but not simpler." The temptation of the wrong sort of innovation is easy to fall for. This type of innovation allows even the most resource-intense and technologically sophisticated organizations to unlearn even the most basic abilities, such as how to make an airplane fly. Consider the F35 fighter jet, an airplane with an estimated lifetime cost of $1.5 trillion. After nine years of continuous delays, the aircraft was still not operational for combat. The aircraft had simply been made too complicated for it to work as it should. For example, there are 24 million lines of computer code just for it to fly. There are few systems in the world more complex than this aircraft.

Malcolm Gladwell argued in The Tipping Point that when any division grows beyond the approximate size of 30 people working together on a particular project, the links between them become too complex for the minds of individual members to process effectively, and the returns and efficiency of collaboration suffer as a consequence.

Following this logic, when an organization grows beyond a certain size, group belonging becomes too diffused and diluted for members to relate to and value each other and the organization. When shared interests and a sense of joint responsibility disintegrate, we become willing to enrich ourselves at the expense of the collective, while causing corresponding harm to it. As such, the end product of communism and capitalism appears ironically similar in terms of the effect on organizational behavior.

We fall down this slippery slope because of our relentless pursuit of economies of scale. Somehow, the way that large organizations adopt many disadvantages of scale is suppressed. For instance, consider the sharply diminishing rate of return for each additional employee once a certain threshold in size and scope is passed. Look at the overall lack of meaningful innovation at companies such as Microsoft, Sony, or Nokia. Though many people believe otherwise, it is not as simple as not being hip enough to attract the best people. In other words, the problem is simply that they have attracted too many people!

COLLABORATIVE DIS-ECONOMIES OF SCALE

Narrow-mindedness and self-interest will always guide organizational behaviors and decisions—it is unavoidable. All that can be influenced is how shortsighted and destructive it is allowed to become. Artificial bloating of revenues to misrepresent growth and profitability prospects in order to mislead investors or short-change employees, partners, or clients have become viable business strategies, all at the cost of sacrificing goodwill and trust.

We are all members of the species called homo economicus; we act according to what offers the best rewards for our expended efforts. In every sphere of modern economics, our desire to contribute Minimal Input for Maximum Gain is morally justified regardless of the damage to the social fabric of trust and solidarity it causes.

A paradox exists: we see ourselves as rational and logical thinkers and yet, in a large enough setting, we will choose to sabotage ourselves and the group we are in. As I attempt to make sense of this paradox, I have arrived at a theory called Collaborative Dis-Economies of Scale. Specifically, this theory describes how a group growing beyond a certain size will see an increasing number of members shift from prioritizing mutual long-term collaboration to acting with selfish short-term interests.

A good example is when the premium for cheating customers far outweighs any costs from having one's reputation damaged. For instance, a taxi driver that works in a city so large he will never risk having the same customer twice. When the links between people become too spread out and diffused, the sense of shared interests and responsibility disintegrates.

Although it's probably not possible to pinpoint the exact size and density of a population in which this phenomenon starts occurring, it appears to be a law of nature that it will do so once a certain limit has been passed. The mechanisms that trigger this wider decline in our ethics can also be seen in individual organizations when bargepole behaviors increase.

To paraphrase a theory by Wharton professor Adam Grant, people mostly fall into the categories of takers, matchers, and givers. Takers strive to get as much as possible from others while offering as little as possible. Matchers aspire to trade evenly. Finally, givers are those who selflessly contribute to others and are driven more by the intrinsic purpose of their work.

I don't imagine that these character traits are entirely set from birth, but instead, they are largely impacted by environment. I see population size and density relative to available resources and economic growth as the most critical factors. However, in contrast to a macro-societal level, as in a city or region, I see it possible to exert greater influence on a company in a deliberate attempt to shape its corporate culture and behavior.

The way in which different character types are assembled and nurtured in an environment where they best complement and push each other forward is a never-ending puzzle. In fact, this ability determines the strength and survival of organizations. I don't know the formula for success, but too many takers, as in bargepolers, looking to derive value from a diminishing number of matchers and givers has always proved to be a recipe for failure.

THE SOCIETAL COSTS OF AN EXCESSIVE BARGEPOLE FOCUS

Economist Joseph Schumpeter popularized the term creative destruction to describe a process whereby economic values and power structures created by previous companies and laborers were destroyed to make room for something better. Regardless of the intentions, the obstruction of the disruptive forces of entrepreneurialism that capitalism promotes tends to hamper innovation and job creation.

The extreme of Bargepole Theory is the diametrical opposite of this continuous rejuvenation and progression. Instead, when participants' priorities are focused on protecting privileges in existing hierarchies, economic development stagnates.

Bargepolers will often be in organizations that run an overall profit. Under certain circumstances, the methods of bargepoling maximize utilization of resources. While bargepolers may be superfluous in terms of the (non) function they fill, companies cannot survive unless the number of bargepolers is limited.

However, this limitation is not applicable in the case of government and non-profit organizations where the vast majority of them make a contribution that is net negative to society. In plain English, many of them steal money and cause more problems than they solve. Obviously, there are a few exceptions.

However, the wealth and welfare of a people or nation is in no way guaranteed from establishing a certain political system built on democratic principles and free-market capitalism. As demonstrated in this book, bargepoling is a force too powerful for any system to be impervious.

How a nation and its people fare is primarily a matter of the priorities they choose to pursue and the ideals that its culture promotes. Herein lies the destructive force of bargepoling when practiced excessively; bargepoling poses a risk of not only being counter-productive but also outright tipping over and sinking entire societies.

For example, Great Britain has shifted from efficiently allocating resources and focus that resulted in the invention of photography, television, and the computer. These technologies laid the framework for the knowledge, media, and digital sectors— possibly the most profitable industries today. However, these inventions were well over a half-century ago. Today, it seems that innovation in Great Britain is less prevalent. The focus seems to have firmly shifted from nurturing the world's most ingenious engineers to educating the best bargepolers, such as bankers, lawyers, state bureaucrats, and advisors. Many of their largest banks have either collapsed or been outright nationalized in order to survive. The value and job creation that these professions have contributed to Britain's economy overall, in comparison to its legacy of scientists and engineers, is a net negative.

These observations are valid across much of the US and Europe today and are no different from the excessive bargepoling that led to the fall of the Soviet Union. In other words, the dominant sector that attracts the best and the brightest individuals is essentially counter-productive.

Usually, nations stagnate or are incapable of developing positively because of their primary national industry being dominated by bargepolers. Instead, these nations should be promoting those people who can contribute with activities that create value. The resource curse, also known as the paradox of plenty, is when an abundance of natural resources, such as minerals or oil, hampers economic growth because the focus of human and financial resources has been diverted to areas that are economically static. In extractive economies, rewards are divided according to bargepole skills to outmaneuver competitors for positions in a hierarchy and not by a person's ability to create value.

This exact same phenomenon occurs when non-value job roles in government agencies or non-profit organizations merely contribute with symbolic value, become better rewarded, and are more desirable than jobs in value-creating sectors.

The best example of this phenomenon is depicted in the aid industry that has come to dominate many African nations' economies. Such aid has completely burdened these nations and had stopped them from living up to their potential.

Africa's long history of aid dependency can serve as a valuable lesson for the destructive practices of a bargepole market. Dambisa Moyo, who Time magazine listed among the world's 100 most influential people of 2009, stated the following in an interview in connection with the release of her book Dead Aid. "In 60 years, we have had over $1 trillion in aid go to Africa [...]. In the 1970s, Africa had 10% of its population living in poverty; today that number is over 70%."

The way these figures have been calculated may be a matter of dispute. It is however difficult to dispute that the aid industry is counter-productive to its purpose and mission by its mere existence.

In Moyo's harsh critique of aid to African nations, she highlights how it primarily supports the lifestyles of 500,000 people working in the aid industry, with most money going to Westerners. Seen in isolation, this example is a good illustration of the bargepole approach and structure.

The same mechanisms that apply to Africa also apply to Europe. Those people creating the idea of a problem needing to be solved are also selling its solution. The most lucrative lines of work are in bargepole organizations that are, in effect, counter-productive to their stated cause.

I can perversely see the aid industry as a metaphor for the economic actors in the West. Europe's countless EU and government representatives that hold cushy and secure jobs are its aid workers. The corrupt dictators are the equivalent of the economic elite in the West, effectively ensured to stay in power by the structure itself and through control of the majority of wealth and resources.

When those people responsible for managing and developing a country appear to be rewarded better for their failures than for their successes, these misaligned interests ensure that no progress is actually achieved if those in charge benefit from the status quo. This principle also applies to many of the businesses active in places such as present day Iraq or the Democratic Republic of Congo. Huge profits are made not only from exporting natural resources, but also from importing goods with the numerous layers of merchants taking their cut along the way. The business of providing security for the safeguarding of supply chains often costs more than the actual product sold. Combined with the difficulties involved for outsiders to enter the market, this situation results in decreased competition and increased margins for those players in the market.

Obviously, it is not a case of an active conspiracy to uphold the status quo of perpetual insecurity in dangerous markets such as in Iraq and in the Congo. But where would you ever expect to find any organization or employees able or much less willing to eliminate their jobs and benefits by making themselves obsolete? Yet, such a case is exactly what is expected from these bureaucrats who inhibit economic development from occurring naturally through market forces.

However, it is difficult to change a system from within until it self-destructs. While not directly transferable to the private sector, there are many valuable lessons to be learned from studying the bargepole techniques used by professionals in non-profit organizations and bureaucrats in the public sector.

BARGEPOLE LESSONS FROM DIPLOMATS AND BUREAUCRATS

The types of people most likely to use cheap, irritating, and obvious strategies to hide that they are not doing any real work—the kind of work that results in anything useful—tend to be in government, associations, or other non-profit organizations. This observation is particularly true if these organizations uphold no essential or practical purpose of commercial value. The classic advice that you secure your job by making yourself indispensable is the worst advice you could ever give to these people. When there isn't a job to be done, it just doesn't make any sense!

Being too harsh on these individuals may be unfair, seeing that these organizations exist for the sake of bargepoling. As such, the main criterion for landing a job in these organizations is to uphold and perpetuate the mirage of usefulness that they continually project.

Nonetheless, there are many techniques to be learned from how professionals in these fields practice the art of bargepoling. While they are not as easily applied in the private sector, the following outline of their main strategies offers small but valuable lessons in becoming a well-rounded bargepoler..

TOP STRATEGIES OF BARGEPOLERS IN GOVERNMENT AND NON-PROFIT ORGANIZATIONS

1. Always Keep Moving to New Divisions and Positions

If what you do can be summarized, and if you are any good at it, you will be stuck doing it for the rest of your life; you will become a jimpee. When the inverted version of this statement applies, you will be able to keep moving forward as a bargepoler. The key is to keep moving.

Never stay in a job for so long that it becomes clear that you are not actually doing a job! Bureaucrat bargepolers must keep moving. This is the main reason why diplomatic personnel only have two- or three-year contracts. By the time it becomes clear that their existence has no purpose (even to them), moving on becomes a necessity for survival; otherwise, they risk becoming a joke.

In the private sector, this principle is often as applicable, particularly for consultants. In the case of Charles as described previously in the first installment of this book series, he was a master at frequently shifting companies and engagements so as not to be questioned about the actual value of his consultancy services. The same is applicable for most jobs of representative function where moving every few years hides the obvious fact that the job fills no actual value or function.

2. Do not Fall into the Trap of Actually Doing Something

Do not do anything practical!

Do not volunteer any help or demonstrate any practical skill. Don't offer comments on unfinished work. Insist on only seeing finished proposals, and make a broad statement on what can be improved. When required to demonstrate that you are doing some kind of work, the best activity is to execute a reorganization of staff members and their responsibilities. However, such reorganization can be a risk as it can expose the fact that there are no real responsibilities. As such, simply do a seating rearrangement; this action, which is of little consequence, is most advisable.

3. Get Along with the Group and Exclude Outsiders

Publicly-funded employees are able to remain in jobs because they collude with each other and protect each other's importance. If you were able to get a job with the UN or the World Bank, it is clearly not in your interest to make the plain observation that the best course of action is to shut down the department; you understand that such a course of action would cause more harm than good to your career.

Instead, it is important that everyone collectively upholds the fantasy that there is important work to be done that requires very specific expertise. The insiders who have this specific expertise are the only ones who understand the complexity of what is being done; this idea is persistently alluded to within the department. At the same time, this fantasy is safeguarded by being unapproachable and keeping closed to outsiders.

4. Appear Constantly Overworked and Non-approachable

The first thing you will notice with this group of professionals is that they always claim to be overworked from working 12 hours, six days a week. They have a backlog of thousands of emails, and, therefore, they have not yet had the time to answer you. Yet, they will look into it and get back to you immediately after they return from that business trip they are preparing for next week. However, they are currently on their way to their next meeting; they will have their secretary try to schedule you in for a proper catch-up—that is, after she gets back from maternity leave.

After covering business while working in the media, I quickly noticed that there is a stark contrast between successful CEOs and diplomats. These CEOs are accessible, calm, and clearly explain their company's involvements and progress. Meanwhile, diplomats, government advisors, directors of export councils, and other variants of despicable publicly-funded ilk often make themselves impossible to reach by employing secretaries to always claim that they are busy in a meeting.

5. Obscure Any Link Between Job Function and Any Direct Outcome

The people who perform this charade of being overworked do so in such a convincing manner that you can't tell if they have in fact been able to even convince themselves that it their supposed overworked life is actually real.

My interpretation is that many of them are so insulated from the real world, which they realize that they have to be for their own survival, that they have no sense of objective comparison even in their own minds. Individuals in an organization who know they are over-compensated need a high tolerance for keeping their cognitive dissonance in check. An example is writing reports that you know no one reads and are therefore certain to not have even a theoretical impact on anything or anyone.

As a bargepoler, you realize that the absence of a spotlight on your work is to your advantage because you want minimal focus on what you are actually doing. However, when these individuals cannot provide any concrete examples of delivering towards their mission statement, expressed goals, or at all benefit anyone but themselves, it must be clear to them on some level that they are useless no matter how proficient they are in the language of non-substance communication.

FINDING THE BARGEPOLE EQUILIBRIUM

Bargepoling is only sustainable when a company is protected from competition by significant barriers to entry or is not otherwise dependent on consistent innovation to retain customers. For instance, extractive economies dominated by sales of a commoditized resource are particularly affected. Overall, bargepoling works best in a stable market environment with locked-in customers and little industry change. Microsoft is a good example where they can depend on licensing fees with each update of their software regardless of how poorly it works. Bargepoling also works well when the product sold is primarily dependent on branding and marketing. The ideal is when both value of the product sold as well as the specific initiatives to promote sales are impossible to correlate and place an objective value on. An obvious example is Louis Vuitton bags that rarely get updated and have no remarkable innovation in either design or features.

However, in most sectors today, companies are more dependent on a diversity of talents if they are to compete. For talents to flourish, a degree of trust is required to shift from an environment shackled in conformity to one of freedom that makes creativity possible. As with the mastery of any art, power is revealed in one's control without having to resort to frameworks and monitoring. Bargepolers must take advantage of the opportunities inherent in their hands-off management approach. In practice, this principle means knowing how to maintain loose enough reins and power distances that allow creativity to flourish.

THE INEQUALITY ADVANTAGE

None are more hopelessly enslaved than those who falsely believe they are free.
—Johann Wolfgang von Goethe

BOOK III

Blissfully Exploited
Promoting Social Tolerance to Benefit
from the Public's Self-Oppression

THE INEQUALITY ADVANTAGE

INTRODUCTION

BARGEPOLE THEORY AND CIVILIZATION

The notion of a free market is a myth. All markets are shaped by laws and regulations, and unfortunately our laws and regulations are shaped in order to create inequality and less opportunity.

—Joseph Stiglitz

GLOBAL HIERARCHICAL INTERDEPENDENCE

The place of your focus will determine who is defined as a bargepoler and who, in turn, is a firewall or patron. When you view the larger perspective, you will see that Bargepole Management can be applied in the power balance of the globalized economy.

For instance, developing nations such as India and China can be seen as jimpees. The jimpees buy into a false meritocracy about moving up the value chain if they just work hard enough. However, they must first accept that the lion's share of the profits for their work goes to Western corporations and that the catastrophic environmental externalities they subsume are wholly for the benefit of increasing the living standards of Westerners. But the Chinese are happy to play along, and you can hear the siren song sung to them by the bargepolers.

For the last decade, I have heard almost daily in discussions about the shift in power from West to East and the hundreds of millions of people in these "new super powers" entering the middle class. No one questions the fact that middle class for the Chinese appears to be defined as those people having a wage of no more than two dollars a day and living beside the factory where they work seven days a week. Reality does not matter as long as those jimpees keep their heads down, are grateful, and continue to produce!

There is no shortage of commentary on these topics, and the theory of Bargepole Management does not add much new insight to existing literature in describing these macro-economic realities. Common themes in this discussion of structural and systemic inequalities resulting in capitalism and globalization include class warfare, social mobility, market sophistication, barriers to trade, and inherent comparative advantages of national economies.

However, the bargepole perspective can strongly help in understanding how inequalities are created, upheld, and benefit those who are able to set the acceptable standards and shared priorities.

CHAPTER I

THE PSYCHOLOGY OF NATION-BUILDING

WHY DO NATIONS FAIL OR SUCCEED?

This question is often discussed. In recent years, a sub-genre of books and TED talks by authors such as Niall Fergusson, Jared Diamond, and Ian Morris have made claims to having identified the success factors in this regard. The proposed formulae tend to be variations of a framework, whereby institutions shape social environment through education, free enterprise, and incentives where upon success naturally follows suit.

Convenient excuses for the sub-par performance of any country or culture, along with suggestions of possible remedies, are always preferred over discussing the actual root causes. How well is a society able to collaborate with each other in larger contexts? How well are they able to structure themselves by means of hierarchies that are respected and meritocracies where those able to create socio-economic value have sufficient motivation to do so?

It is easy to forget how difficult it is to organize any population beyond a certain size. Wholesale chaos and violent infighting are the norm rather than the exception. Europe is not exempt. Modern history includes wide scale terrorism in Northern Ireland and genocide in the Balkans. Instead of asking why nations fail, it is more relevant to ask the following: "Why don't all nations actively fail?"Inadvertently, once a critical mass of non-discipline is reached among people in an organization, a nation, or a region, it is difficult to turn the tide toward productive behaviors.

Or, for that matter, when groups of bargepolers are able to lay claim to excessive proportions of rewards without any meaningful contribution, the tide is also difficult to turn. Both scenarios will cause societies to eventually fall into chaos and conflict.

When considering almost any Central American nation, whether a democracy or dictatorship, you can easily see how temptations to abuse power for personal benefit ruin their countries. If the leaders knew how to properly bargepole, these nations would be perceived as healthy, and they would demonstrate social stability with GDP growth. This perception would be the case, despite these leaders being equally corrupt and abusing their powers for personal gain. A few examples of nations with leaders who were skilled at establishing functioning bargepole practices include Iraq under Saddam, present day Saudi Arabia and Venezuela under Hugo Chavez.

An Economist review from 2013 of a book on Hugo Chavez summarized the skills of this world class bargepoler: "His response when any problem was revealed was to fire a minister or create a new ministry. Sometimes he did both. He ran through 180 ministers in a decade. [...] Omnipotent or not, Mr Chavez was never responsible. Fellow travellers with the revolution explained that while all did not go according to plan, the commandante meant well. Failures were the fault of corrupt officials who had deceived the great man."

The success or failure of a nation is based on whether the leader's objective for bargepoling is self-serving or utilitarian, and if there is a means to an end to uphold stability. The tricky balance includes not bargepoling too much, too recklessly, or allowing too many people to become bargepolers. The following chapters will demonstrate how social inequalities based on group belonging can be justified when benefiting society as a whole through means of Bargepole Management. The risks involved for excessive bargepoling being rejected and revolted against are also described.

THE SOCIAL HEGEMONY OF THE
BARGEPOLE SUPERSTRUCTURE

Before presenting the societal models based on the theories of Bargepole Management, I must first mention inverted totalitarianism. This established political theory describes fundamentally similar mechanisms for managing the perceptions, values, and behaviors of the US population. The bargepole theories presented hereafter are influenced and built partly on this philosophy.

Inverted totalitarianism was coined by political philosopher Sheldon Wolin, who used the term to illustrate similarities between the system of government in the United States and conventionally totalitarian regimes, such as Nazi Germany and the Soviet Union. The functioning of these government systems essentially strives for the same objectives and outcomes. However, the most apparent difference is how centrally organized public propaganda institutions using coercion and threats to silence opposition have been replaced by a supposedly independent media that instead relies on the appearance of freedom and political disengagement.

Wolin writes that the power of the inverted totalitarian system "lies in wielding total power without appearing to [...] enforce ideological uniformity or forcibly suppress dissident elements so long as they remain ineffectual. [...] The United States has become the showcase of how democracy can be managed without appearing to be suppressed." Wolin continues, "Democracy represented a challenge to the status quo; today it has become adjusted to the status quo." This observation can be seen in how even universities take part in this inverted oppression; they claim to promote critical thinking, but instead, they do the opposite. Chris Hedges also used the term inverted totalitarianism in Days of Destruction, Days of Revolt to describe how citizens are commoditized, exploited, and lured into surrendering their self-interests and political representation in government and being pacified by their consumerism and pursuit of sensationalism. Manufacturing Consent by Edward Herman and Noam Chomsky is another book that makes a similar argument about the illusion of a free and independent media being a part of controlling the populace.

SYSTEMATICALLY EVOCATIVE SUBTERFUGE

The core of any organizational strategy is to establish widely accepted structural inequalities that are neither revolted against nor otherwise demoralizing. Unopposed inequality is particularly critical for a political ideology and leadership to succeed. Herein lies bargepoling's fundamental strength and purpose. In modern-day societies that are very socially connected through media, the strategies used for bargepoling have evolved significantly. The most common and effective strategy for a group to create and uphold inequality that they can benefit from is called systematically evocative subterfuge.

The definition of subterfuge is "to use deception to conceal or avoid something in order to achieve a certain objective." Systematically evocative subterfuge as a form of bargepoling is most clearly seen in the ongoing public battles that involve morally righteous and often polarizing social issues. Whenever there is an overpowering fanfare about a particular issue and its proponents bolster their position with strong emotional arguments, the larger objective is to take attention away from more inconvenient injustices.

For instance, it is safe to rail about raising the minimum wage, to elect the first black president, to allow gays in the military, to increase the number of women on the boards of Fortune 500 companies, or to raise awareness and funds for remote locations struck by natural catastrophe or disease.

Ironically, making progress toward these causes is largely irrelevant to the lives of most of those people who are inspired to care the most. However, many fail to realize that this fuzzy feeling of "doing good" is at the cost of sacrificing their own self-interests because they are distracted. Instead, these efforts are effectively counter-productive as initiatives to forward their own interests fail to be properly recognized and represented.

The practice of systematically evocative subterfuge relies on the ability of those people in power to influence the faux indignation of a group and encourage them to become involved. Eventually, the harmless demands of the group are granted, allowing the group members to experience a fleeting sense of moral superiority from collectively engaging in these issues; they believe that their efforts are achieving progress.

To paraphrase Machiavelli, the masses are impressed by superficial appearances, and it matters less who and what really is. On all levels in society, you can see the practice of this principle. Prevalent examples include the initiatives to cut carbon emissions, to buy fairtrade coffee, or to participate in demonstrations for human rights. Such token initiatives provide the public with the impression of achieving progress, but in reality, it is to distract them from the overall structural inequalities that uphold inequalities and exploitation that go unquestioned. Jimpees play the main part and do the lion's share of keeping themselves in place by forfeiting chances for social mobility. Ironically, this objective is achieved most effectively by getting the jimpees to think that they are doing all they can to advocate change; thereby, they accept the status quo of the artificial power differentials they are living under.

As a bargepole manager in a corporate environment, the practice of this concept on a small scale involves the encouragement of similar token initiatives. Announcing that free coffee will no longer be available to ideally contained within the group. The intention is to draw attention away from systemic inequalities and corruption that is at their expense as a group. Ultimately, the jimpees allow themselves to be subjugated by the bargepolers who grant or deny them these symbolic gestures.

Summarily, irritation is not conducive to teamwork and productivity; an unhappy employee is not one who works hard. However, if you can create small irritations and problems to distract a person, he or she will become more easily manageable, predictable, and ironically enough, more easy to placate in the long run. The trick is to uphold and leverage inequality between the hierarchical layers through consistent distraction from the bigger picture of what criteria is chosen to determine how position and rewards are endowed.

AUTO-DISPLACED COGNITION

We all know the same truth, and our lives consist of how we choose to distort it.
—*Woody Allen*

We live in a time when leaders can be indistinguishable from salesmen. Often, when we decide to believe and support them, our decision is based on emotions that they have inspired in us to serve their interests at our expense. Ideology trumps pragmatism when we accept illogical explanations as the price to maintain consistency in our value system. Exploiting this social weakness is an important bargepole technique called auto-displaced cognition.

Auto-displaced cognition borrows its concept from Freudian psychology. Freud's theory of displacement describes the unconscious defense mechanism of subconsciously refusing to acknowledge certain urges and desires and instead refocusing on something perceived as more acceptable.

In today's age of living in information overload, the skill to create the outline for what is deemed acceptable translates into real power in that it restricts courses of action. By extension, it also restricts the possible outcomes in a way that can be controlled. An interpretation of a situation is presented as morally normative to the public while opposing views are made unacceptable either to promote or to defend. This interpretation is then sold as accurate on the basis of public perception alone by an artificial consensus forced on the public by its continued repetition of a chosen narrative.

In short, auto-displaced cognition is the theory outlining the process of how this phenomenon occurs and how it can be used by bargepolers to broadly create the backdrop for what gets considered acceptable to discuss and what comes to be seen as reasonable opinions and points of view. First, a problem is oversimplified and framed in moral and sentimental terms. This oversimplification obstructs critical and comparative evaluation and suffocates other issues that are preferably avoided. Second, biases and even vested personal interests are masked by obfuscating and pointing out a correlated matter that is made to appear as though it cancels out the unsavory situation or otherwise makes it an unavoidable side effect. In the final stage, an accepted understanding is reached in the public consciousness. This understanding occurs when it is insensitive to point out obvious root causes to problems or conflicts of interest. It is then forgotten that those made responsible for solving the problem were also the ones who created it, oftentimes from thin air.

Examples of this technique's use can be found in the flawed logic that was accepted to justify the Iraq invasion in 2003, the domino theory of the Cold War, the new economy of the IT bubble, the Y2K bug, the subprime mortgage crisis and the trade of carbon credits. In each of these cases, those people creating the idea of a problem needing to be solved were also selling the solution to fix it. Recommended reading for an expanded view on this concept is Naomi Klein's The Shock Doctrine: The Rise of Disaster Capitalism.

SYSTEMATICALLY EVOCATIVE SUBTERFUGE AND AUTO-DISPLACED COGNITION IN PRACTICE

The main mode for leaders of political and interest groups who practice bargepoling of larger populations is to engage in the previously described techniques of systematically evocative subterfuge and auto-displaced cognition.

By establishing protective walls around themselves, bargepolers avoid scrutiny. The two techniques are particularly effective in areas where political correctness is rife. Anyone who dares to question fundamental inconsistencies in a leader's arguments or points out root causes that are being ignored, will find themselves under attack.

In the psychology of bargepoling, pushing on sensitive nerves involving "correctness" is done to the fullest extent possible, and playing these cards correctly is an invaluable tool for deflecting accountability, or rather, non-performance.

This matter is complicated by how the parameters and definitions of morals are arbitrarily defined by context, group dynamics, and collective perception. Whereas one group or one person's actions may be deemed as unethical, the same actions by another are seen as virtuous. This idea is most clearly demonstrated by how a society and culture make a group share a common opinion and understanding of their history and identity.

A case in point is the firebombing of Tokyo that was unnecessarily barbaric and lacked any real military objective. With the scope of the death toll and the indiscriminate targeting of civilians primarily, the event can even be classified as genocidal. Yet, most people are unlikely to have heard the term genocide in connection with this event; in fact, many people may be unaware the event even happened.

In the Academy Award-winning documentary The Fog of War, Errol Morris interviewed former US Defense Secretary Robert McNamara, who participated in the planning of the Tokyo attack. McNamara stated the following in reference to the firebombing:

"We burned to death 100,000 Japanese civilians in Tokyo—men, women, and children.... [US General] Lemay recognized that what he was doing would be thought immoral if his side had lost... But what makes it immoral if you lose and not immoral if you win? LeMay said, 'If we'd lost the war, we'd all have been prosecuted as war criminals.' And I think he's right—and I'd say—we were behaving as war criminals." This example demonstrates how on a large scale, the meaning of actions and their consequences can effectively be influenced after they have occurred.

This is by emotional considerations being made to trump objective evaluation, or even any recollection at all, of the facts.

In order to be successful and profit from the bargepole practices of auto-displaced cognition and systematically evocative subterfuge, everyone must be made to accept an established moral consensus in which self-interests are seen as rightfully pursued and maximized.

The way that bargepoling uses moral arguments to avoid objective comparison and scrutiny is often so well done that it can be difficult for the public to even recognize. Two different yardsticks are openly used and accepted as justified.

An example of this strategy is found in the phrase, "It's a matter of education." Specifically, this phrase is used to support a lack of evidence and illogical reasoning for a certain problem. If you don't nod in agreement, the price paid is being shunned and labeled as intolerant and bigoted.

Over Easter weekend 2014, 45 people were shot in various spontaneous shootings in Chicago alone. About a hundred shootings took place in that two-week period. This did not stand out as a tragedy and barely received any media attention. No serious discussion was held on the endemic problem of inner-city violence and its root causes of broken social norms. No one recognized the death toll to be on the level with a war zone, nor did anyone suggest that the UN or a similar organization be sent to Chicago to try and maintain order and safety for the people. The best to be expected would be various coded phrases that seek to excuse or justify these incidents and behaviors among the social groups they occur.

The manner in which problems such as these are addressed has nothing to do with actually examining their causes or solving the issues. The debates never directly acknowledge socially attributable root causes or confront the self-serving political agenda that is the underlying motivation for the discussion itself.

Other hot topics that are used in the US to polarize and pit conservatives against progressives include abortion, gun rights, recreational drug use, and homosexuality; all of these issues are part of the so-called "Culture Wars." These debates are deliberately framed as moral and ideological, so the issues cannot be resolved through compromise and reason. As Sheldon Wolin indicated in Democracy Incorporated: Managed Democracy and the Specter of Inverted Totalitarianism, "Their political function is to divide the citizenry while obscuring class differences and diverting the voters' attention from the social and economic concerns of the general populace." This concept is related to bargepoling by analyzing those people or groups whose interests are served from consciously controlling the public's reaction (or non-reaction).

A seemingly different discussion, but one that is an example of the same form of bargepoling in action by the food industry, is found in the way obesity is discussed in America. Clearly, most obesity is caused by the commercial interests to promote vast intakes of industrially produced lard and sugar. Overwhelming availability and aggressive sales tactics crushes the willpower of people to resist. Yet, seriously addressing the problem or proposing any realistic and practical solutions is conveniently evaded with that same one-liner intended to espouse sophistication, caring, and tolerance, "It's a matter of education."

Consider how ridiculous it would be to actually ask obese Americans if the reason for their obesity is a lack of education. Could the concepts of nutrition somehow have escaped them? Are they unable to grasp how tons of lard and sugar inserted into your mouth each year leads to obesity? Yet, many obese people will readily agree that they in fact lack knowledgeabout a healthy diet and are thus blameless. In a perverted way, oppression with the pretext of tolerance is more effective than any other form of coercion. When people accept absolution through a lack of self-accountability, which in turn is neatly packaged as an expression of freedom, the potential threat that the will power of the public could pose to the established order, is neutralized.

The best way to oppress any person or group is to let them oppress themselves without realizing it; you can even make them think that it is for their own good. First, this scenario makes for a large group of jimpees that are subjugated by a wide power gap to the bargepoling classes and, thus, are controllable and non-threatening. Second, if you can make money from these people's self-oppressive behaviors, this is an added bonus. Jimpees are most easily incentivized with instant gratification. This concept has certainly not escaped the bargepoling classes in society that are profiting in the form of jobs created in its wake. In fact, this scenario unfolds not only in increased sales of consumer goods, but also in government-funded social programs as well as platforms and agendas for politicians on both sides of the political spectrum. Ironically, by doing this, the perceived relevance of these politicians is raised in the eyes of voters.

The individuals and groups who practice this deliberate distortion of problems do so in order to serve their own interests. They are not motivated to actually address root causes that would solve the real problems. Again, in what industry would you ever expect to find any organization or employees able, much less willing, to eliminate their jobs and benefits by making themselves obsolete?

In the case of political and social matters, this situation would demand that short-term incentives are created to counter the daily behaviors and decisions of individuals acting self-destructively. However, as indicated earlier, this idea directly opposes the objective that Bargepole Management Theory seeks to achieve by benefiting and securing the bargepolers in their positions.

Further examples of how these tactics are pervasive throughout society can be observed by analyzing the function of today's media. Addressing actual issues is always conveniently avoided, if not completely ignored. The job of the media should be to make important matters interesting; yet, just the opposite seems true. One could deduce that the West's definition of freedom of speech is now no more than the packaging of cheap entertainment. Debate, analysis, and independent thought have been boiled down to being either for or against irrelevant matters presented on grounds that are purely emotional, with the personalities of news anchors being the primary attraction.

Instead, people allow themselves to be tranquilized by their insatiable thirst for spectacle, celebrities, and scandal. In the US election process, the catchy one-liners from the candidates and putdowns of their opponents seemingly make out the foundation of the parties' entire political platforms. These practices cast doubt on how highly the prized cornerstones of democracy are actually held, much less practiced.

The public's disinterest to distinguish relevant and factual information from controversial statements made for entertainment purposes strips them of the ability to have any meaningful impact and influence on the conditions and circumstances that shape their lives. This blissful ignorance of the masses is not as innocent as it is often presented.

The North Korean public gets duped with fantasies and is denied knowledge about the problems facing their country. Meanwhile, westerners voluntarily ignore that the lines get blurred between what is real, relevant and true from that which they deem amusing. It is seen in how the media covers the relatively minor threat posed by fundamentalist terrorist groups in remote and inaccessible locations while largely ignoring the barrage of serious crimes committed by illegal immigrants in practically every neighborhood across America. Focusing attention on fabricated events and hyped up societal problems is at the cost of ignoring actual problems that directly affect us every day. In that case, how is propaganda in North Korea any better or worse than what gets practiced in the West? From this perspective, it would seem all that is required for succeeding as an African-American, for instance, is to live up to a standard that is generally accepted as being absolute minimal for any person born healthy with average intelligence.

Of course, this is a presumptuous statement to make. Regardless of the parents' background, culture, and intelligence, when raising a child in an impoverished area with widespread prevalence of drugs and gang crime, it is impossible to control the outcome. It is absolutely nonsensical and pointless to seek explanations or speculate about any correlation between self-sabotaging social behaviors and the ethnic composition of a group of people.

What is critically relevant, yet largely ignored, are the deteriorating social norms that the American population at large is encouraged to accept rather than combat. The consequence is that the overall potential and opportunity for self-improvement are significantly restricted among the general population.

A fair question is: What does the US bargepoling class stand to gain by weakening the standing of the nation overall? However, this is to miss the point as their aim and objective is to protect a position of unfair advantage and to leverage benefits regardless of how well the organization is doing as a whole.

If you listen to the political debate in the United States today, the bargepoling class is at constant war to justify how extreme inequalities are not only deserved but are a requisite for a healthy and competitive economy. The defense of capitalism is that self-interest leads to the benefit of all. Yet, in the case of the many corporate breakdowns and financial crises in recent decades, it has not even been a zero-sum game but a negative-sum game. That is, the gains by the winners are less than the losses suffered by the losers.

While this may seem quite cruel to suggest, the most painful is that the masses of jimpees fail to realize that they, behaving as individuals and as a group, are both the cause of their problems and the main barrier for improving their situation.

THE PYRRHIC VICTORY OF MEDIOCRITY

The American dream used to be that if you worked hard, success was accessible and rewarded fairly on a level playing field. Now, there is a consensus that rewards are not distributed fairly and there is no clear connection between work and reward. As such, the American dream had to be redefined as one where mediocrity can triumph from time to time. Having to work at all for reward is missing the point completely!

From this perspective, it is easy to understand the appeal that Barack Obama had to the American jimpee population that elected him president. Just like any commercial for a get-rich-quick scheme, part of the pitch to vote for Obama was to let your children know that becoming president really was within their reach—granted, of course, that they can learn to mumble a selection of platitudes from a teleprompter. The same can also be said about the wide appeal that Sarah Palin had to many. This is in stark contrast to how no American seriously believed they, too, easily could have been JFK, Nixon, or Reagan if circumstances in their lives had been different. The exceptional personal qualities that each of these men possessed, and that made them what they became, are impossible to deny.

Many remarkable aspects of Bargepole Management Theory are present in the flock psychology around Obama, which explains how he inspired the jimpee populations not just in America, but around the world. Most significantly, what separated Obama from other unknown charismatic leaders that have risen to power in history was how his mediocrity was a central component to his appeal rather than a handicap to conceal or a barrier to overcome. All the while, many of the wealthiest Americans complain about their government and the inefficiency of the political system. Nonetheless, they are the only ones benefiting from the default position of a status quo preventing any fundamental structural changes to how power and wealth is distributed.

55

AUTO—DISPLACED COGNITION AND SYSTEMATICALLY EVOCATIVE SUBTERFUGE ON A GLOBAL SCALE

If you can't make it good, at least make it look good.
—Bill Gates

Jimpees' susceptibility to auto-displaced cognition and systematically evocative subterfuge is clearly seen in how they prioritize supporting popular ideas and movements over more pressing problems that directly affect them.

For instance, why is there such a focus on relative fringe issues such as HIV and starvation in Africa when there are far more people dying from diabetes and heart disease caused by overeating? Yes, diabetes and heart disease killing more people than AIDS and starvation hold true even in Africa and across Asia. However, aid organizations aren't creating posters of some fat kid looking helplessly into the camera with the following tagline: "For less than the price of a cup of coffee, give this obese child a heart transplant, a new liver, and a bit of liposuction." Meanwhile, malaria and diarrhea have exponentially higher death tolls than HIV, and both of these conditions are more easily and cheaply preventable.

These are examples of how auto-displaced cognition is applied in practice. The latent and constantly present threat of being labeled as intolerant in some way is the main tool and enabler. Problems are neatly packaged with a thin veneer of politically correct platitudes that is part of an overall agenda to distract and obstruct critical thinking. This thin veneer shields the actual problems as well as whose interests are getting served versus sidetracked or ignored.

Framing issues in moral terms consistently distorts the overall ability of jimpees to apply critical thinking. In turn, bargepolers are able to easily force more irrational arguments on jimpees, thereby making them accept unfair circumstances and actions taken against their interests by distracting them with matters that are ultimately irrelevant to them.

So how is this done, and who is benefiting?

If you think auto-displaced cognition is a kooky idea, think back to the Live 8 concerts that were held simultaneously in eight cities around the world in the summer of 2005. With Bono as their "spiritual leader," masses of jimpees gathered to espouse their collective wisdom on economic policy to pressure the world's leaders in connection with the G8 summit being held. The message was largely the same as it has always been and still is: increase aid dependency and offer broad debt relief—at the expense of taxpayers! A cruel irony that is lost on these jimpees is that Bono, along with the other members of U2, pay almost no taxes in their home country of Ireland and engage in highly complex tax planning.

It should come as little surprise to discover that Bono's pal, Bill Gates, along with Warren Buffet and Ingvar Kamprad (founder of IKEA), are also masters of practicing auto-displaced cognition. These three men have all been crowned and have been taking turns being named as the world's richest man. These men have skillfully sold the idea that they as individuals, as well as extensions of their companies, are inextricable from the business of philanthropy. In the case of IKEA, the company is even established as a charitable trust. As for Warren Buffet, he is spearheading a PR campaign for billionaires to publically pledge, non-bindingly, that they will donate most of their wealth to charity at some point in the future. Bill Gates is a supporter, and he has even managed to convince jimpees to donate money to a foundation bearing his name! You can imagine how hard Bill probably laughs at this when he hosts his parties. As The Economist noted, "Bill Gates was once vilified as a modern robber baron before he transformed himself into the world's greatest philanthropist."

The reasons why these men would be motivated to practice bargepoling toward the jimpees in this world should be obvious at this point. Yet, just to reiterate, the way they constitute the practice of bargepoling and auto-displaced cognition is how they have jimpees waving their hands, jumping up and down, and cheering on the inequalities that they are perpetuating and bearing the brunt of.

The theory of auto-displaced cognition and how it is used to manipulate people in modern-day societies builds on the work of Wilfred Trotter and Gustave Le Bon. They wrote seminal works on the social psychology of how the herd instinct is present among humans and how propaganda is used for its influence.

But a more familiar comparison with auto-displaced cognition is George Orwell's concept of "doublethink." This concept is the act of ordinary people simultaneously accepting two mutually contradictory beliefs as correct.

Orwell described doublethink in the following passage in his book 1984: "To know and to not know, to be conscious of complete truthfulness while telling carefully constructed lies, to hold simultaneously two opinions which cancel each other out, knowing them to be contradictory and believing in both of them, to use logic against logic, to repudiate morality while laying claim to it, to believe that democracy is impossible, and that the Party was the guardian of democracy."

THE INEQUALITY ADVANTAGE

CHAPTER 2

JUSTIFYING THE BENEFITS OF GLOBAL INEQUALITY

The secret of life is to appreciate the pleasure of being terribly, terribly deceived.
—Oscar Wilde

The growth of nation's population and GDP determines the increase in its share of consumption of the world's resources and its toll on the environment. It is politically insensitive to suggest that billions of people in developing nations should be denied development for the sake of our planet's greater good. Yet, we look favorably on a growing middle class in developing nations despite it being starkly incongruent with our undeniable interests of maintaining our living standards and avoiding environmental catastrophe.

What is fair in this question is highly subjective. One could rhetorically ask why any culture should be entitled to benefit from, much less strain the environment with, energy that demands technology they have not contributed to developing and are unable to supply or sustain for themselves. As the old adage goes, a bird cannot rise too high if it is by the strength of its own wings. Inversely, as seen in the urbanized environments of third-world cities, no culture can sustain a level of sophistication that it does not itself live up to.

Irrespective of what lofty morals we want to believe we have, it is clear that our objections to benefit our own welfare, at the expense of other people, rarely go much beyond our urge for the new iPhone or MacBook. As long as the factories are not in our own countries or do not employ workers that look too similar to us, we will not give it much thought.

That we disingenuously pretend to have solidarity with all people equally is dangerous, if not outright counterproductive. It prevents us from seeing, much less dealing with, the bigger problems at hand.

Only five percent of the world's population enjoys life with the comforts and conveniences we in the west take for granted. The brutal reality is that in order for this richest five percent of the world's population to maintain their living standards, the absolute majority of the world's population is required more or less to settle for their currently small consumption and not expect significantly more. Inequality is nothing new, and mankind was not designed for voluntary self-sacrifice. Though we shy away from admitting the reality of these intrinsic qualities in ourselves, dealing with them is the key to our long-term survival, and a degree of inequality between nations and people is inevitable. Negotiating this order and dividing resources, peacefully or otherwise, is what civilization has always been about. Relative poverty of the many is a natural consequence for wealth to be enjoyed by the few. This is bargepoling on a global scale.

Striving to move the world's population toward a distribution of resources and consumption that is even remotely equal, and thus seen as fair, is not a viable option. Leaps in technological innovation will not be able to magically lift the living standards of the world's poor. More efficient use and generation of energy will not solve our energy problems. This can be seen in how coal makes up 70 percent of China's power generation and is its fastest-growing source of energy in real terms. Comparatively, with the exception of nuclear, increasing the efficiency of coal plants is more effective in counteracting environmental destruction than the realistic potential of increasing all presently used sources of renewable energy.

A sensible definition of fairness could be that no person, group, or people should rightly consume more value than it is able to create; likewise, each group should be responsible for what it has created. Viewed this way, a rational conclusion would be that a large proportion of inequalities between people and nations are naturally justified.

The problem is that the system is broken. It is seen not only as a reasonable model wherein everyone is rightfully entitled to more than what he or she contributes; it has become the only morally valid and acceptable model to support, at least superficially.

It is plain for any person to see that this is an utterly absurd aspiration to have. We all know this, whether intellectually or on an intuitive level, yet we refuse to acknowledge it openly, even to ourselves. This is why, without fully realizing it, we all engage in everyday bargepoling. For the most part, we do this through token gestures that make us feel as if we actually care. When you hear a phrase such as "need to raise awareness," "being part of the solution and not the problem," or "it's better to do something than nothing," it is a case of bargepoling, only this time by the jimpees, using the technique called symbolic gestures of tokenism to uphold and morally justify massive discrepancies in power in order to harvest the fruits of privilege that it brings.

SYMBOLIC GESTURES OF TOKENISM

Consider how hard it is to find anyone who doesn't support basic human rights or who is not against the destruction of nature. Yet, it is big business to get the public to feel a need to pay for expressing these values through symbolic gestures of tokenism. The motivation for claiming to represent such a cause is to obtain the moral license to do what you otherwise could not justify. This rationale explains initiatives that are logically incompatible—exotic adventure vacations to environmentally vulnerable areas to raise money to protect rainforests somewhere else entirely, for example. Or loan sharks operating under the guise of being aid workers giving out microcredits to rural women in third-world countries, so they can set up stands to sell Coke and Mars bars. Daring to question the moral legitimacy of any of these feel-good movements makes you feel evil. This is due partly to our all being in on these schemes and benefiting from them.

Token initiatives are acknowledged as largely ineffective but appear at least to serve a purpose by bringing attention to various issues and taking steps in the right direction. To misrepresent why actions are taken, and in whose interests, is usually either counterproductive to the claimed cause or a distraction from the interests that are really being pursued.

Tokenism is the most effective tool for upholding systemic inequalities and deficiencies that favor a group that doesn't want attention drawn to it. Tokenism is everywhere. The real change Obama delivered was to free people with a credible alibi for their true feelings about black people. Salad is the most fattening diet in the world as it is used as the prime excuse to eat cookies and ice cream. Supporting renewable energy initiatives is the token license that frees us from those nagging voices in our heads while we take thirty-minute hot showers.

Engaging in the symbolic gestures of tokenism is our excuse to avoid the unpleasant actions necessary to deal with or even acknowledge a problem or situation. When we interpret issues as part of a group, our objectivism is handicapped by collective emotion. What appears to matter is not always real, and that which is real is ignored. We prefer to accept reasoning in line with what we want to believe as a group. Sometimes, we are manipulated to surrender our own best interests to benefit others. Sometimes we manipulate ourselves to find shelter from truths that disturb us, and as a result we refuse to see the connections between cause and effect that are right in front of us.

Breaking away from these shackles requires actual awareness, which involves seemingly counterintuitive interpretations of motivating factors. Much of what we see as intelligence is the ability to separate emotion from fact. Much of understanding is seeing how the two are never fully separable.

HYPERBOLIC DISCOUNTING AND SELF—SABOTAGING BEHAVIORS

Economics can be seen as an extension of sociology and psychology. More specifically, it is the scorecard of the aggregated incentives upon which a group acts. Economics reveals a story that cannot be understood if separated from either sociology or psychology.

As such, practically every problem in society is behavioral at its root, and the solution is found in changing counter-productive behaviors. The obstacle for changing such behaviors is that the doctrine of personal freedom, democracy, and capitalism are used interchangeably to promote and justify jimpees to continue with their self-sabotaging behaviors. They are lured to sacrifice their best interests for future wellbeing in exchange for fleeting luxuries.

This is the point where former totalitarian regimes ultimately failed. These regimes directly and actively oppressed the masses and limited their freedoms, but they irrationally believed they could still motivate the masses to work hard without commensurate benefit to themselves.

Yes, democracy and capitalism are largely responsible for increased welfare and decreased conflicts through the spread of free enterprise and trade. Yet, the main enabler of these effects has been this reinvented form of oppression that can be explained through the models of Bargepole Management Theory. Bargepole techniques, such as establishing false meritocracies, limiting of communication, and obscuring information, uphold power to exploit the naive layer of jimpees making up the bulk of members in any hierarchy.

The bargepole approach has enabled modern capitalist democracies to succeed by keeping power structures stable with the help of self-oppressing spending patterns by the majority of its citizens. That is, people voluntarily sacrifice opportunities for long-term benefits and chances of self-improvement in exchange for satisfying momentary urges. A good example can be seen each morning in cities where minimum-wage workers wait in line to buy expensive takeaway coffee.

This behavior can be understood by studying the concept of hyperbolic discounting. This concept describes people's willingness to pay a premium for immediate versus future rewards. In its inverted form, the opposite also applies, as people are willing to accept disproportionately higher risks and costs if there is a time lag for paying them. For instance, imagine if the consequences of smoking and sun tanning were immediate; if conditions such as cancer materialized instantaneously instead of with a delay. The reckless engagement in any of these activities would probably be as uncommon as seeing anyone running across a crowded highway with speeding traffic.

However, our own best interests and long-term future wellbeing are sacrificed in exchange for a consistent trickle of token rewards that offer us comfort and distraction. These token rewards are the currency that jimpees are incentivized with most effectively.

Compare this scenario to previous examples of Bargepole Management Theory applied in companies with social manipulation as well as social engineering of the work environment. The jimpees are motivated by false meritocracies and controlled through the four-layer bargepole hierarchy where communication is restricted, information obscured, and token rewards offered.

For both citizens and employees, consumerist ideals of pursuing instant gratification unite the masses. This predictable and consistent behavior among jimpees keeps bargepolers safe from accountability as they take the credit and the lion's share of rewards while minimizing exposure to risk and the value of their contribution. What separates the bargepolers from the jimpees is a deeply internalized sense of superiority that allows them to stand above the masses to resist giving in to sudden urges and to remain focused on maintaining a longer perspective of achieving their objectives.

CONFLICT AVOIDANCE

As mentioned previously, most conflicts, whether in society or in the workplace, are more emotional than practical at their roots. As flock animals, we as humans are vain in nature and easily manipulated. We are largely unaware of how our thinking can be distorted by status, prestige, and rewards. Making people feel that they deserve more and better, as well as that others are unfairly taking from them what should rightfully be theirs, is simple. It is difficult to make people feel they have what they deserve. It is easier and more effective to dissuade people from making direct comparisons in the first place.

Whether in a democracy or in a dictatorship, maintaining stable conditions is usually the result of clear power differentials and social demarcations at large. The best example is a monarchy where the subjects do not question the fairness or logic of inherited wealth and power that stem from the people. Religion with its notion of determinism, the creation of social classes with hereditary inheritance, and, more recently, the belief in the meritocracies of the free market with equal opportunity for all, also display basic concepts of the philosophy of Bargepole Management.

However, the ability for a nation to practice Bargepole Management is becoming ever more complex, and many nations have recently been failing spectacularly. An explanation for such failure is found in the deterioration of traditional religious beliefs and social norms in modern societies. Respect for established social institutions is withering. As such, modern bargepoling is not only more difficult but also ever more critical. In the absence of a unifying religious dogma, the function of Bargepole Management has grown increasingly critical for minimizing conflict between groups in societies. Put plainly, bargepoling needs to create power differentials that help avoid direct comparisons between groups and the questioning of structural inequalities.

The US has been the most successful society in this effort in how they built an illusion of the American Dream being within reach for everyone on equal terms. However, just as the dictators in the Middle East have started struggling with upholding the fantasies they are projecting, the ability to exert control on populations and influence them in any direction is being lost. Instead, the illusions of false meritocracies are rejected, and entitlements and privileges are seen to be unfairly distributed. The fallout is a situation where people are less controllable and more difficult to motivate and manipulate.

CONFLICT AVOIDANCE VERSUS CREATIVITY

There are many factors that can explain a country's economic success. Innovation explains prosperity for many nations, yet it is an insignificant factor for the majority of countries. Singapore is often used as a prime example of a country successfully creating prosperity. Their main accomplishment has little to do with innovation and everything to do with creating social stability despite their extreme ethnic and religious diversity. This ability is the most significant and universal factor predicting a nation's development. It is like a teacher getting the class to sit down, be quiet, and pay attention; there is no single correct way to accomplish this feat. However, if a teacher lacks this ability, the investment in more textbooks and computers in the classroom will not compensate for it.

A more homogenous composition of an organization's members may cause less friction as a result of fewer misunderstandings. Groups may be effectively segregated to minimize opportunities for conflict. This idea is perceived to be at odds with how a diverse workforce, made up of people who complement each other in their thinking and work well together, will lead to greater creativity and thus innovation.

However, I see these matters as separate, and, therefore, they should be treated as such. The complicating factor is that we tend to overlook or deliberately ignore when and where innovative thinking and creativity is important. We must consider if it is a greater priority than the benefits gained from having more control over workers' social environments.

A modern trend is to overstate how companies in today's economy, and especially in the future, will compete in having the most innovative ideas. As such, the priority is to find the most creative individuals and to get them to work together. This flawed assumption stems from our wishful thinking of how we want the world to be.

Even in professions where you would think creativity is priced at a premium, it is often secondary. Consider much of the media industry around the world. Finding photographers who show up on time, bring the right equipment, and work fast is often a larger concern than their creative skills. The same is often true for journalists, where having a high quantitative output, getting along well with co-workers, and interviewing subjects frequently makes up for a complete lack of originality or analytical skill. Creativity is often mistaken for merely having the wherewithal to see what needs to get done and not leaving it half-finished.

The group dynamics of people working together is inevitably influenced by co-workers' backgrounds including culture, education, ethnicity, age, gender, religion, and even their hobbies. These factors fundamentally have a bigger impact on how well a group functions and performs compared to any corporate culture; the corporate culture is designed to shape and establish values to deliberately inspire a certain group behavior.

With obvious exceptions such as Research and Development (R&D) in technology and medical fields for instance, an environment with the absence of conflict between workers matters more than creativity in terms of the results of most companies and societies at large. Consequently, confrontations are actively suppressed or deflected. This occurs not necessarily due to a lack of differing views and interests but by simply being avoided. It is here that effective Bargepole Management and social engineering of the environment influences how corporate cultures can achieve these objectives.

In hindsight, it was a convenient lie that individual inventors and leaders brought us forward in giant leaps. For instance, the idea of inventors spawning ideas from scratch in "eureka" moments is a misperception. Even Alexander Graham Bell's telephone and Thomas Edison's lightbulb were the results of broad incremental improvements in an era where innovation over long periods enabled such paradigm shifts.

In reality, individual willpower is very limited in a larger perspective. How well an individual performs in society and how society fares as a whole are almost completely dictated by societal structure as well as its established norms, expectations, and accepted behaviors. Though many people prefer to identify themselves as rebels, humans are hardwired by nature to be herd animals. We simply do not dare to deviate that far from the group.

On this note, our separation from animals is not through any willpower to go against our environment. The way one civilization is able to develop and outperform another is how we as humans are able to consciously and purposefully design, influence, and set the norms of accepted behaviors for the group. To paraphrase Confucius, all men are created equal; it is their habits that distinguish them.

OPPORTUNITY IN SCARCITY

Indisputably, corruption and lack of transparency have stagnated economic growth in many of the nations experiencing civil unrest. When corrupt governments are replaced by democracies, the hope is always that bribery, cronyism, and embezzlement will be rooted out from the everyday lives of people and business environments. This belief in the power of democracy goes hand-in-hand with capitalism, further ensuring transparency and free competition. However, the correlation between democracy and lesser degrees of corruption is neither obvious nor automatic.

In some cases, the impact of democracy could be argued as merely broadening the base for corruption from the concentration of individuals among the political elite. While discussing the merits of democracy as an ideology is irrelevant to the purpose of this book, I make this statement simply to warn of idealized expectations about sudden and radical improvements in market efficiencies.

To quote Thomas Edison, "Restlessness and discontent are the first necessities of progress." However, when restlessness and discontent are the consequences of overwhelming jealousy and envy, it is a recipe for downfall.

Meanwhile, proper Bargepole Management is both insurance for and an antidote against this scenario.

During much of my childhood and youth, I spent a great deal of time in both Singapore and Chile during periods of strong economic growth. What I saw were built-in safety mechanisms that prevented societal inefficiencies from taking root; the safety mechanisms were central to both of these nations' success stories. Fundamental parameters were in place to restrict public servants from abusing their positions; they were unable to create obstacles and delays to obtain bribes. Overall, opportunities for parasitical behaviors were deliberately minimized.

As an example, one of the first things I noticed when arriving in Santiago was how most stores, small or large, only had a single person who was allowed to accept payment. In other words, only one person handled the cash register. Even buying a piece of gum at a pharmacy required three separate people to give pieces of paper to each other before the goods were finally handed over to the purchaser. In Singapore, getting fined for spitting out gum on the street is as insignificant as it is illegal to bring a single pack of gum into the country.

According to Transparency International, both countries have long been among the least corrupt countries in the world. In the context of Chile widely outperforming its Latin American neighbors, and Singapore's unique position in Asia, this lack of corruption is particularly impressive.

It is irrelevant to ask whether these countries have populations with more evolved morals and characters. Character is not revealed in what a person can restrain him or herself from doing in any given situation. Instead, such restraint is largely dictated by the aggregate of life experiences and the given circumstances at hand. A person's authentic character is best revealed by how they would act if they knew with absolute certainty that they would not get caught. As such, among many populations, advancing in economic prosperity will not require more opportunity but less.

With today's economic growth and job creation, an unfortunate paradox exists in that companies have a better chance in appealing to our bad habits for the sake of indulgence. Consider that when we live in the habitat for which our bodies were designed with six hours of movement each day and an all-natural diet, the norm is to have the physique of a professional athlete. Our failure to live up to this natural state of being is explained more by our unnatural opportunities not to, rather than any individual strength or weakness of willpower.

The same logic is easily applied in understanding how the economic health and efficiency of societies are a reflection of the standard culture sets; similarly, it is a reflection of acceptable social norms and behaviors. Only allowing for opportunities to engage in activities that are not counter-productive for the group or self-sabotaging to individuals can be seen as a formula for social progress and personal wellbeing.

THE INEVITABILITY OF BARGEPOLING

"Strive not to be a person of success, but a person of value."
—*Albert Einstein*

In summary, systemic failure and inefficiency occur when too many people in a society are bargepolers or when political leaders in a society bargepole too much. In these cases, the masses (jimpees) fail to see the purpose of trying to become anything other than some form of a bargepoler. Either as a government bureaucrat or businessperson, both positions are seen as being gained by dishonest, if not criminal, methods. The connection between working and creating real value in order to be rewarded is not sufficiently established or recognized.

It is not corruption so much as sheer "leechism" that explains why nations fail to create overall prosperity for their people. When I lived in Jakarta, I was told it was an open secret that jobs as public servants in positions to take bribes were sold to the applicant able to pay the most. These economically counter-productive "jobs" were often the best paying jobs available. It may sound provocative, but it is a simple observation that various forms of leeching, on all levels of society, are the national industry of most countries that remain poor. In fact, these countries remain poor despite having favorable conditions to promote prosperity, such as natural resources, access to education, and a functioning democracy.

Excessive bargepoling in many nations has caused a general lack in understanding the connection between values created by a person or a nation and what such values can be exchanged for in the marketplace. Many national populations experiencing political upheaval, such as Egypt and Libya, suffer skewed perceptions of themselves that obstruct them from dealing with reality. Too many populations have outlandish ambitions and expectations of receiving phenomenal compensation for very little effort.

There is an overwhelming trend to speak obsessively about the move toward a knowledge economy that will dominate the future job market. However, when considering the US, a majority of the unemployed have some form of college education, and Department of Labor statistics estimate that seven out of ten growth occupations over the next decade will be in low-wage fields, such as service jobs.

This observation is not pessimistic. Instead, it is a reassuring outlook at the world's economies; the demand in the market remains centered on the need for people to simply do things that need to be done. The fact that nobody is particularly thrilled about having these jobs does not change this reality. The countries that are able to act on delivering a "value economy" and do not focus solely on the pipe dream of a work force in the "knowledge economy" will have major advantages in being able to create the most valuable asset of all: social stability through means of gainful employment.

In comparison to previous generations, current generations no longer have a strong correlation between working and surviving. For an ever-growing global urban population, the basic human needs of survival are met. Most people can afford coffee in the morning, transportation in motorized vehicles, cigarettes, and smart phones. Significant improvements in lifestyles and personal wellbeing require a radical increase in spending power. However, instead of this scenario being something positive, it is proving to be a cause for social incitement and upheaval around the world.

Maslow famously argued in his Hierarchy of Needs that once a person is able to fulfill their basic needs they aspire to self-actualization. Now that the fight for survival has largely been removed, it is having the ironic implication of becoming another human tragedy. Our essential needs are no longer earned; instead, such needs are provided and are now expected as if they are a minimum human right. Meanwhile, self-actualization is being confused with fulfilling impulsive urges for the consumption of luxury goods. Together, this situation is fueling an existential angst in that we no longer have clear answers as to the why and what of our lives.

Attainment of happiness is not what gives us satisfaction; indeed, our pursuit of happiness is what is gratifying. If this idea is so commonly agreed upon, why is it being ignored? While it may be controversial to postulate, is not the value and product of a population's work activities secondary to providing a task to fulfill? Isn't there significant importance in working as a form of duty that offers a sense of purpose, identity, and self-worth? If you disagree, you only need to look at the consequences we see in pursuing the opposite.

Expectations that are in line with our achievements, and feeling a degree of control in influencing this balance, are central elements to our sense of justice and personal satisfaction. I see these elements as the most valuable consequence of what is commonly perceived as freedom and democracy. In other words, a world where rewards are neither random nor dictated by favoritism! When considered from this perspective, any group, regardless of their relative affluence or welfare, can be made to feel disadvantaged, dissatisfied, and oppressed. It is achieving the opposite that is difficult for a leader to inspire in an organization.

The teachings of Bargepole Management Theory, its approach, and how it is practiced go beyond political, moral, and religious beliefs or values. No one is consciously in favor of increasing inequality. But what many fail to recognize is that the problem is not inequality in and of itself. The solution for overcoming inequality is not reduction; instead, we must know how to manage it, how it is perceived, and how to best take advantage of it.

The objective of Bargepole Management Theory from a societal and macro-economic perspective is to generate gratitude among the masses who unwittingly but voluntarily encourage the inequalities that disfavor them through their self-sabotaging behaviors and inability to set long-term priorities. Thereby, consumer spending and minimal wages maximize economic growth and activity. Social stability self-perpetuates as a natural consequence.

In the end, the Inequality Advantage taking root is inevitable. There is no viable option or escape from Bargepole Management being applied and eventually abused in society by individuals, organizations, and governments. Thus, the only questions for each new era, generation, or civilization are the following:

What should it be called?

How are the rules of engagement for bargepoling drawn up?

MINIMAL Input MAXIMUM Gain

Bonus Material

BARGEPOLE MANAGEMENT

The Art of Getting Priced at a Premium

"A RARE GEM" - Forbes

MITCH VANDELL

Bargepole Management

We are what we pretend to be, so we must be careful what we pretend to be

—Kurt Vonnegut

TABLE OF CONTENTS

PREFACE: YOU TOO CAN BECOME A BARGEPOLE MANAGER!

AUTHOR'S NOTE

INTRODUCTION TO AND OVERVIEW OF BARGEPOLE MANAGEMENT

BOOK I:
CREATING YOUR UNFAIR ADVANTAGE

CHAPTER I:
LEARNING FROM THE MASTERS

CHAPTER 2:
THE SELF-ACCEPT PSYCHOLOGY

CHAPTER 3:
THE ECONOMIC PRINCIPLES OF BARGEPOLE THEORY

CHAPTER 4:
A HOW-TO GUIDE: IMPLEMENTING THE BARGEPOLE STRATEGY

APPENDIX:
THE PSYCHOLOGY OF COUNTER-POSITIVE THINKING

Bargepole Management

PREFACE

YOU TOO CAN BECOME A BARGEPOLE MANAGER!

We are all pursuing success. Many books sell the idea that there is a secret to being unveiled in this regard. These books appeal to so many people because they suggest shortcuts from the long, hard, painful, and most of all boring expenditure of time, effort, and repeated failure required to achieve results.

The brutal reality is that few have what it takes to be the best or even partially good, for that matter, at anything. I don't state these views to discourage or demoralize you from trying to achieve your goals or succeed well above your potential. No, I am telling you this for the exact opposite reason! I am here to tell you that there is a shortcut those other books have not described. You have witnessed this shortcut your whole life. It is bargepole management theory.

It has nothing to do with improving your professional skills to deliver any kind of measurable results. It will not help you become a better person or improve your ability to sell more or work harder. In fact, substantially improving yourself and your situation through willpower, positive thinking, or the law of attraction is futile. Instead, this book will teach you the infinitely more valuable approach of taking credit for the work of others while remaining insulated from accountability—and reaping the rewards.

Bargepole Management

AUTHOR'S NOTE

Theories on how privileges are built up and protected in society and in the market place are common. The focus of this book is on finding the corresponding principles that apply to individuals within a single organization.

My inspiration to write this book first came when working on a project that involved several hundred people over an eight-month implementation period. After it was completed successfully the head of the organization congratulated us and requested that we replicate it for a neighboring province in the next three to four weeks. Never mind that the logistics and permits alone would take months, the specialized equipment had to be custom made and local personnel would need recruiting, but the campaign itself was not even relevant in any other location. It suddenly dawned on us, as he was taking credit for the recent success, he did not even have a basic understanding of the nature or the scope of the work being carried out.

In recent years we have seen how no senior banking officials acknowledged mistakes leading to the subprime mortgage crisis in 2008. Those at the top not only escaped punishment, many were rewarded. Similarly, no one took responsibility for the colossal miscalculation of the costs for invading Iraq. How it is possible to fail catastrophically yet maintain a reputation of being successful and competent is a central theme in the pages ahead.

I have worked in and observed various industries and markets under dramatic circumstances. Shortly after graduating from university I was on location in Indonesia when the Tsunami struck in 2004, and supported rescue workers with the delivery of communications infrastructure. In the lead up to the global financial crisis I was at the Financial Times in London before moving to Dubai in 2008 for a front row seat of the boom and bust of their real estate market. In the years that followed I visited Baghdad repeatedly at the height of the insurgency, saw the first elections in Kabul after the war and was invited to visit Libya shortly before the fall of Gadhafi.

My experiences over the years from varied contexts in different cultures have led me to identify many destructive patterns of leadership styles that maximize personal reward. But the more interesting aspect of this is how, in certain social conditions with the right balance of hierarchical inequality and lack of transparency, these same behaviors can counter-intuitively maximize the results for an organization as a whole. I hope you will enjoy this book and that it will challenge you with new perspectives and insights.

INTRODUCTION TO AND OVERVIEW OF BARGEPOLE MANAGEMENT

> Bargepole: A long pole with a hook used to push or pull boats in and out of a dock slip in a harbor. The word is commonly used in the expression, "I wouldn't touch that/him/her with a bargepole."

Most of us, especially if we've worked in a corporate environment or a large government body, have experienced a feeling of injustice when a superfluous leader without skill, knowledge, or value is the best rewarded. In those cases even the mailroom clerk thinks he could do a better job than the boss. So why do we make up excuses for why we haven't made it to the top of the pile?

We live in an age where practically anyone, regardless of background, can rise to the top of any public or private organization. That is good news. Even better, no superior performance, legitimate professional skills, intellect, or ability is necessary to achieve these positions. These days, achieving success in almost any organization is largely a result of successful packaging, self-promotion, and outmaneuvering colleagues who vie to climb the same corporate ladder as you.

We've all heard the advice, "fake it 'til you make it." But with so many fakers, what separates the few that actually make it to the top tiers of their profession without demonstrating any discernible value or skill? Most who fail overpromise and make claims that get exposed as inaccurate. In contrast, those who succeed are like diplomats: everything is left open and unsaid. They are above reproach and paid lavishly, and they don't get fired for underperforming.

The way these individuals advance in a corporate hierarchy beyond where their competence or skillsets should take them is rarely a coincidence. In short, the answers are found in the theory of bargepole management, the recipe for the new American dream: minimal effort and skill for maximum rewards and adoration. It explains how individuals as well as companies and groups within societies can benefit from the inequalities and lack of transparency they are responsible for creating.

A NOTE ON THE STRUCTURE OF THIS BOOK SERIES

In essence, bargepole management theory allows people to create inequalities and to uphold and benefit from them by suppressing overall transparency. Learning the methods for practicing bargepole management begins by looking at individuals and their behaviors in organizational contexts. The theory is then applied to relationships between companies on a corporate level. Finally, in the last installment of the series, the approach is discussed on a global economic scale and how it relates to political systems of nations.

The different perspectives of the theory will be covered in the following order:

- Bargepoling as it affects and is applied by individuals in organizations.

- Bargepoling and its impact on organizations as both a competitive advantage and a liability.

- Bargepoling applied to the governing of nations and global politics seen in the context of human nature and civilization.

Bargepole management theory is a standalone management philosophy but can also be seen as a reference and complement to helping one understand the ulterior motives of existing management literature.

THE FOUR-LAYER BARGEPOLE HIERARCHY

Most central to bargepole management theory is the construction of the four-layer bargepole hierarchical structure. The first layer is the power patron, who grants a bargepoler a position of power in the second layer. The third layer is the firewalls who effectively function as scapegoats. The final layer is the jimpees (derived from useful idiot workers).

The expression useful idiot describes naïve people who are lured into supporting movements they don't fully understand and may even go against their own best interests. While leaders despise them for their ignorance and gullibility, they cynically exploit these useful idiots to promote their agenda. The term is often used in political contexts, and while its origin is debated, the concept can be traced back to the early days of the Soviet Union and its use of propaganda.

The term useful idiot is transferred to bargepole management theory, where junior staff members in organizational hierarchies are called jimpees. The ideal jimpee is easily manipulated, at least initially, to accept large amounts of work with little compensation and buys into vague promises of future rewards and promotions.

Once you have identified a patron and secured the foundation for a bargepole position, bargepoling largely entails suppressing competition within the organization to defend the carved-out territory. This is the function of the four-layer bargepole hierarchy, wherein you create artificial power distances to insulate and grant you unfair advantages in an organization. Its primary enabler is how it allows the bargepoler to influence and restrict communication flows between the hierarchical layers, thereby controlling the perceptions of the various groups.

THE FOUR-LAYER BARGEPOLE HIERARCHICAL STRUCTURE

1. Patron (e.g., company owner or board director)

2. Bargepole manager (e.g., senior manager or director)

3. Firewall (e.g., line manager or team leader)

4. Jimpees (e.g., operational and frontline employees)

THE LARGER PERSPECTIVE

Depending on where you place your focus, a bargepoler can simultaneously be the firewall for the patron. This duality continues up and down the organizational structure. It is common for numerous bargepolers to exist within each hierarchical layer, as bargepolers bargepole other bargepolers. In other words, there are times when you may be the bargepoler and other times when you are the cannon fodder on the frontline or even the scapegoat.

When you zoom out completely and view the larger perspective, you can see how bargepole management applies to the globalized economy. For instance, we can see workers in a developing nation such as China as jimpees. Under the guise of moving up the value chain and improving their future prospects, they accept the brunt of environmental destruction and brutal work conditions that foremost benefit the corporate interests and living standards of people in the West. China's elite class is the layer of firewalls. Members of this class are paid enough to push forward and enable the human and environmental exploitation while also serving as scapegoats that absolve the bargepolers (the West) from their moral culpability for the benefits they reap from these activities.

The United States is another example of bargepole management theory in action in a macro perspective. The United States overtook Great Britain as the dominant political and economic power in the twentieth century largely due to its lack of a regimented class society or bargepole hierarchy. The social and political order of the United States primarily favored the interests of the broad middle class, and the best could succeed regardless of their backgrounds.

Ironically, these typically American hallmarks have been inverted to instead create the ultimate bargepole hierarchy. These macro perspectives of bargepole management theory in delved into in 'the Inequality Advantage – Principles of Covert Power' that demonstrates how inequalities are created, upheld, and benefit groups within a society and even shape hegemony between nations.

Bargepole Management

BOOK I

Creating Your Unfair Advantage

Bargepole Management

CHAPTER 1

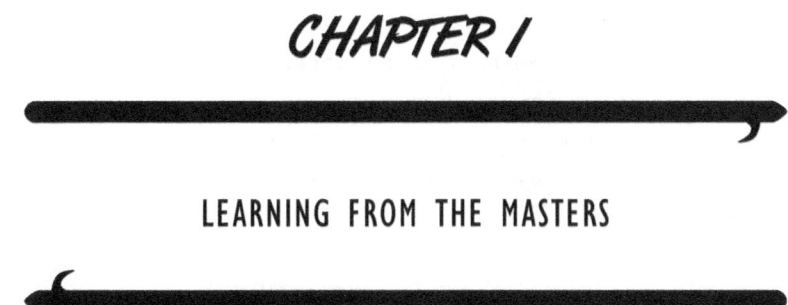

LEARNING FROM THE MASTERS

Before I get into explaining the theory and its practice in detail, let me begin by telling you three stories that demonstrate three main types of bargepole managers that showcase different aspects of basic bargepoling in action.

The three fictional characters—Dave, Charles, and Bill—represent distinct personality types that are able to build careers completely on carefully crafted façades and social maneuvering. Judging from their appearances, they seem to be counterparts, yet they have built their careers firmly through the mastery of bargepoling. Their most valuable skillset is their ability to sell in high expectations and projecting an image of being critical members of the organization. Their method for achieving this is based around the objectives to:

- ▸ Detach performance from any quantifiable measurements
- ▸ Motivate others to accept accountability and to forfeit the credit and rewards for their work to them
- ▸ Control communication between the layers of an organization to present information in ways that best serve their self-interests

Warning: As the typical traits of bargepoling are surprisingly clichéd, some readers may believe that these stories are based on either them or bosses they have known. While these types represent aspects of practically every known bargepoler, let me state clearly that these following characters are entirely fictional and based on a mix of hundreds of nameless men and women around the world. The stories are in first person solely for the sake of narration.

TYPE A: THE ARISTOCRAT

THE STORY OF DAVE — THE IMMACULATE DIVISIONAL DIRECTOR

To demonstrate how the four-layer bargepole hierarchy functions in the real world, allow me to introduce you to Dave, an expert at using the bargepole hierarchy to practice control over who can communicate with whom. Jimpees are kept from understanding the bigger picture of organization's hierarchy while senior management is kept from seeing the real causes behind failures. A relative isolation of groups to disconnect open communication between them is central to shielding his limitations from being exposed.

Despite working for the company for more than ten years, very little background was available on him. Not even the people who knew him from the time he'd started had been able to glean any significant information. The best intel on his background was that he had been an actor of sorts. He had played a role as an alien that had no dialogue in a big Hollywood disaster movie. With the makeup and the gills on his neck, it was difficult to be certain if this alien was actually him, and nobody dared to ask.

Dave had cemented his position in the company by entering the organization early, deeply mining a few sources for his power, and designing the perfect bargepole hierarchy to protect himself. In this particular company, Dave was not alone in this description; in fact it was valid for most of senior management. However, Dave was the best at shrouding himself in a superior and mysterious façade in order to create distance from any direct operations; he insulated himself from failure. His appearance was immaculate, and he spoke in a deep, slow, and superior tone of voice. I would sit in meetings with him and just admire his act. It was a perfect mixture of refined culture, class, and sophistication designed to make people assume it had been shaped over generations by attending private schools in the English countryside and perhaps marrying into royalty.

Those of us who had experience with the real deal could, of course, tell that Dave wasn't authentic. There was definitely no academic background, serious analytical ability, or creativity in any of his ideas. Everything he said was completely unsubstantial. But non-substance communication is central to avoiding discussions where there is a risk of being asked to clarify details or delve into the reasoning behind a position or idea. Dave was a master at this. He relied on stating universal truths in the form of observations of known facts or statements on values, goals, and aspirations. These were usually intended to be non-sequiturs, so the discussion would conclude with the idea that he had offered leadership and direction.

Body language and intimidation make this non-substance communication technique possible. It helps to be tall, have a large build, have a deep voice, use a sophisticated vocabulary, or have an upper class accent. The key is to gain any type of psychological edge so as to intimidate colleagues and control interactions with them. In this way, it is easier to steer conversations by asking leading questions, so as to produce the desired type of answers. Likewise, discussions can be framed to touch only upon simple matters with little need for interpretation.

Dave's common preference was to focus on basic things, such as payment terms on a contract or the price and quality of inconsequential services or products being delivered to the company. Another example was his establishment of procedures whereby numerous signatures were needed, most importantly his, to execute simple purchases. This made him appear busy and important, since he was signing papers and granting permissions. It also perpetuated the avoidance of having to make interpretations and decisions he would be held accountable for and have difficulty justifying. More importantly, it shielded him from the risk of revealing his lack of understanding and competence.

While Dave could be described as an imposter of sorts, his social intelligence and discipline were certainly genuine! These critical skills, required for bargepoling, may be easy to understand in theory, but they are difficult to emulate unless you have the talent. Even upholding a naturally dominant posture and never revealing doubt or nervousness in your voice requires enormous focus and consistency. As I studied Dave, I couldn't help but be overwhelmed by how perfect a fake he was. Indeed, he was so perfect it wasn't really relevant that he was a fake.

While most organizations would see an annual staff turnover of nearly 50 percent as a problem, Dave viewed it as an important element—indeed a requisite—of upholding his image and career. The important thing was that his critical firewalls didn't leave him. They were less interchangeable and more risky to replace than the jimpees. But even these firewalls were not indispensable.

Dave's skillful designing of the perfect bargepole hierarchy, complete with firewalls and jimpees behaving in predictable patterns, was his real achievement. His position was so protected, it did not matter that colleagues and fellow managers from other divisions saw him as an actor who added nothing to the table. Nobody could remotely determine what he did besides signing off on expense claims.

The joke about Dave was that he would look himself in the mirror each morning and ask himself if this was the day he would be exposed as a fraud. But the joke was really on those making it. It didn't matter that people knew he was really an imposter. Like the natural evolution of Jay in The

Great Gatsby, Dave was impervious to being discovered. He was a man who had far overreached his potential and social background with a façade and position so perfectly crafted, it was simply accepted at face value. He could walk down the corridors and speak like a man of royal descent, and colleagues would literally bow their heads.

In a sense, it must be argued that overreaching your potential and the public's expectations is the purest and highest form of success. Given this, Dave was the most successful man I have ever met. He was like a one-legged man competing in the Olympics. Compare this principle to sons of great thinkers or industrialists; they may perform well above average expectations in their careers, but they are still seen as failures because of the potential they are presumed to have, considering genes, environment, and opportunities handed to them.

Skilled bargepolers like Dave often reveal themselves by talking about having "the right amount of carrot and stick" and being "process oriented" and by outlining KPIs that need to be met, which they follow up with in the form of detailed reports that include statistics. The motive behind these bargepole techniques is to claim credit regardless of the outcome or to preemptively create a convenient alibi in case of failure. He can show the KPIs, targets, and procedures were perfectly planned and in place, but the individual jimpees and firewalls failed. This is done as if to say, "If only they had listened and done what I had said and what they had agreed to." Even though these exercises are transparent and are obvious ways to avoid being cornered on any actual contribution, they are effective means to obscure the lack of any meaningful expertise.

A bargepole manager like Dave critically understands the limits to his or her knowledge, skill, and ability to influence specific or overall outcomes. Therefore, a skilled bargepole manager like Dave chooses to focus on what can be described as a mix of cheerleader and quality controller.

This is not to say that cheerleading and quality control are not valuable and useful functions for a manager. However, the bargepoler projects these qualities as being central to the functioning and strategic direction of the company.

TYPE B: THE ENCHANTER

THE STORY OF CHARLES — THE 'I'M MORE THE IDEA GUY' CONSULTANT

On the surface, Charles built his career on simply mixing buzzwords like thought leadership, innovation, empowerment, and sustainability into every other sentence. However, there is much more to his phenomenal success story.

Charles is the opposite of Dave in how he comes across to people. He's an entertainer, industry expert, and everyone's close confidante. His talent for becoming 'best friends' with everyone he meets is creepy. People just simply want to know him, be of help, and see him succeed. And best of all, he has the magical gift of not making people feel jealous of him. He just makes people feel good and avoids objective comparison as well as evaluation of his actual skills and contributions. Charles is also the type of person you would describe as genuine, honest, and straightforward, only to later realize that it is all a conscious act as a means to an end.

A person who is generally upbeat with positive energy and spirit is usually preferred over cynical individuals with a bleak and realistic outlook. Never underestimate how people want to believe and follow individuals who are optimistic. Enthusiasm trumps substance when people become willing to put rational and critical thinking aside.

To be clear, in the case of bargepolers like Charles, he possesses a kind of artistry and skill that is practically impossible to learn unless you have a natural flair for it. A central tool for this charade is humor that is tailored to each person and situation. His humor is contagious and disarming, and it makes people feel good and not want to criticize him or what he's saying. He lights up the room and makes people feel as if they are the center of attention. He is able to uniquely understand them and share common insights on every topic that is important to them.

By being vague and favoring open-ended commentary, Charles avoids candidly expressing his reasoning and risk getting exposed with embarrassing gaps, or seeming gaps, in his knowledge. His perfect execution of simply noting general trends, reiterating the arguments of others, or pointing out plain logic, he appears to offer substance and insight to the discussion without the addition of any original thinking or information.

Charles' skill takes years of close observation to even realize that he is putting on an act – all of the time. While it may seem that the bond is built on a strong foundation of mutual understanding and loyalty, it suddenly dawns on you that he is actually not expressing any opinion or information of substance. When you reflect on his statements, while seemingly insightful and full of conviction, you realize that these are observations or opinions that would be irrational to argue against.

In his early childhood, Charles immigrated with his mother to South Africa as she realized that the class system in their home country of England would be a disadvantage to him. After dropping out of high school, Charles dabbled as a singer and radio disc jockey before randomly finding his way into the banking sector. It could have been practically any sector, as these consultant-type bargepolers all operate with the same tools of personality, charisma, and personal favors from friendships to get ahead. By sheer 'coincidence', he became friends with the son of one of the directors, and he was accepted into the family's inner circle who worshipped at the synagogue on Saturdays. Soon, people in the industry simply assumed that he was Jewish, related to the banking family, and educated to some degree at a top school, none of which he ever needed to clarify.

I had known Charles for many years, and I heard him skillfully deflect questions about his educational background numerous times. I later found out that he had dropped out of high school. In all the time I had known him, I had assumed he had an MBA from an Ivy League school. Never would I, or anyone else for that matter, have thought he was a high school dropout.

As you can imagine, Charles' ability to sell himself as an educated expert to a field of bankers with highly technical knowledge in finance is quite impressive. That being said, Charles was no slacker in reading up on theory, and there was probably not a single aspect of finance in which he could not pose an intelligent question or make a relevant comment. While it may appear difficult to spot these types of bargepolers, they are revealed in that they never present an analysis that can be refuted or offer opinions that go beyond widely agreed upon observations.

When Charles moved to the Middle East he conveniently dropped his charade of being of Jewish descent and started consulting. His first order of play was to get in with the CEO of one of the big financial firms and secure the title of 'Director.' Armed with this title as well as his assumed authority, expertise, and influence, Charles solicited consulting gigs all over the region, mostly on the golf course. It was incredible to see how there was not a single field of finance in which he was not an expert. It didn't matter if it was something as disparate as legal compliance, futures, risk-assessment, HR-practices, or IT systems; Charles spoke as a world- renowned expert, and people listened.

To pass himself off as a financial expert by just parroting others and hide his lack of any meaningful contribution demanded social sway with influencers. With the credibility they offered to the wider groups, no one had any interest or incentive to see through Charles' bullshit. In fact, any attempt to do so would be a risk to their own standing and reputation with these influencers on whom they also depended. And while many experts realized that he had no actual skill or knowledge, they still enjoyed his company enough to play along and not question him.

Both Dave and Charles are character types that represent world class bargepolers. It can also be concluded that these individuals could easily be removed from the organization without having any direct impact on performance in terms of productivity, strategic direction, or anything else. But more significantly, they are masters at maximizing gain from minimal input.

In the case of Dave and Charles, they often inspire both great awe and ire in how they are like shells; it is impossible to know what, if anything, is inside. In some cases, their act is so convincing that it can take years of working with them to realize that you don't actually know them beyond their surface.

Bargepoling is often achieved by acting out a role, convincingly and consistently. You might be able to fake an Oxford accent. If you are extremely good at faking the accent, you might be able to pass as being from Oxford for a little while. However, it would be very difficult to convince someone from Oxford that you were actually born with the accent. Therefore, if you are going to fake an Oxford accent, you'd better do it outside of Oxford, and you'd better not stray from faking that accent! This example is only one of countless others where self-discipline for upholding an image is a part of successful bargepoling!

TYPE C: THE TYRANT

THE STORY OF BILL — THE BULLYING SALES DIRECTOR

A less apparent bargepole manager and the least sophisticated of the bunch is the bullying type. The best example I have seen of this was Bill. He had the good fortune of being one of the first employees at an English publishing house that launched in the early nineties in Kuala Lumpur. His timing was impeccable, as Southeast Asia was then in a period of explosive growth.

If you met Bill, it would be an absolute mystery to you, as to how he'd ever gotten involved in sales at all. The man was indescribably rude and inhospitable, bordering on violent. He was the kind of person you would pay not to deal with as a boss or as his client. A persistent rumor was that he had been to jail for some crime before moving away from the United Kingdom. Picturing him with his pent-up aggression in any kind of drunken brawl, like a football hooligan beating someone up, wasn't very difficult.

Despite his personality and appearance, Bill was the man in charge. Absurd as it may sound, I often heard colleagues say, "Bill is the only one who can get the results," to justify his position in the company.

On the other hand, this was hardly surprising seeing that no sales representatives good enough to get any other job stayed on to work under him. That meant the lifespan of a new staff member was rarely more than six months. Ironically the better someone performed, or the more potential they showed, the less likely they were to stay on. Bill made sure no one had sales figures that could in any way threaten his standing as "million-dollar Bill"—a nickname he alone used for himself.

From the day a new employee started, Bill made it clear that the only clients they could contact where those no one had reached out to before. This meant that it was essentially impossible to find clients to sell to. There were countless big companies that had never booked any ad campaigns with the publishing house and had not been contacted for years because they shunned Bill. Even so, selling to them was not permitted. If questioned on this, Bill would claim he was currently in the final stages of negotiating a million-dollar deal. Considering there had never been a million-dollar deal in the history of the company, it was surprising that he could say this with a straight face on an almost weekly basis, "Million-dollar Bill has a million-dollar deal on the table." His limited vocabulary consisted mostly of monosyllabic grunts that went well with his oversized figure, which resembled a mix between a gorilla and a bull. This came in handy for intimidating colleagues who objected to him.

In the rare cases where a member of the sales team would close a major deal with a client, Bill would stand by and watch the team member do so before informing that he was taking the commission for the sale. He would predictably claim that he had in fact communicated with the company at some stage in the last decade. Time and again the sales representative in question would protest loudly before resigning in disgust. On two occasions I saw Bill offering to settle the dispute with a fistfight. He must have been surprised when both accepted his challenge and even more surprised to get knocked out twice! Both times he immediately fired the employees. The result was always the same, with the unanimous conclusion that Bill was the only one who could "bring in the figures."

Bill eventually got fired in the midst of the Asian financial crisis. If I remember correctly, his wife left him the next day, with their newborn baby, as he defaulted on mortgages for a luxury villa and an Italian sports car that was subsequently repossessed. While I cannot imagine any punishment severe or cruel enough for someone like Bill, there was at least some satisfaction in seeing that in the end he had nothing to show for his many years of what can only be described as hard and ungrateful bargepoling work.

LESSONS TO BE LEARNED

I am sure you too have encountered personalities like Dave, Charles, and Bill, and don't aspire to be anything like these exaggerated stereotypes, who are unlikely to enjoy much personal satisfaction or professional pride.

It is possible, however, to be a bargepoler without making it known to people in your environment. With a sufficiently unclear job function and results that are difficult to measure, it is possible to be liked, have respect, and be seen as a hard worker who is in charge of extremely important matters that are often conveniently too complicated to understand or that you are not at liberty to discuss.

The advantages of getting into a bargepole position are manifold. But the question remains: what can we learn from the stories of the bargepole masters? By aiming to teach you how to maximize your compensation with minimal input, studying these men is a good start toward understanding how bargepoling works in practice. This book is a guide for becoming a bargepoler, but its purpose is also to offer insight into how many modern bargepolers function, their motivations, and the reasoning behind their behaviors.

If you exclude the countless state bureaucrats and NGO workers, very few people, in relative terms, are able to become highly rewarded bargepole managers in private enterprises. Reality dictates that those shrewd enough to succeed as bargepole managers are unlikely to need this book in the first place.

Regardless, if you have what it takes to be a successful bargepoler, you will almost definitely have to deal with a bargepoler at some point in your career. Usually you will encounter a bargepoler as your boss. By getting along with your boss and understanding how to best collaborate, you will be able to make the best of the situation.

Whether you are a jimpee doing the actual work or a firewall that provides cover as a scapegoat for the bargepoler (e.g., team leader, divisional head, or deputy general manager), this book will help you maximize the benefits of your position. It may feel highly demoralizing to answer to a bargepoler. Nonetheless, having one as a boss can have many benefits, especially if you are able to understand what freedoms are possible and how you can take advantage of them.

In the world of hierarchies, it is natural for people not to be content with their present position and to desire to move up the ladder. They feel as if they deserve something better, although the specific position of their boss may not be what they want. If you can't beat the bargepoler at his or her own game, you must consider how to take advantage of the way bargepole organizations benefit you.

This book will make you more aware of the rationales and reasoning of bargepole managers so that if you answer to one, you will know how to avoid being taken advantage of for the gains of others. The examples will help you cope in organizations that are rife with bargepoling by demonstrating how relationships with powerful bargepolers can best be handled. Instead of sucking up to the boss, the better strategy is to have the boss perceive you as valuable to his or her image. Most important, you must not challenge your boss directly to gain any advantages nor indirectly to benefit any of his or her challengers in the organization.

On the opposite side of the spectrum, this book also sheds light on behaviors we universally see as negative yet rarely confront. Exposing these behaviors and making them more recognizable can serve company owners well if they wish to minimize bargepole behaviors that are counterproductive to their aims for the organization.

WHAT MAKES A BARGEPOLER?

Bargepolers have always existed, and they are always evolving. Yet, it is fair to say that Bargepoling is more prevalent now than ever before. For example, you find it common that employees often struggle to explain what they do or give any example of being of use or financial benefit to anyone except themselves.

Government and non-profit organizations such as associations and NGOs are often more prone to Bargepoling than privately owned companies exposed to competition. Professions that are particularly suitable for Bargepoling are those in which the pricing of services is based on perceived intangible values rather than quantifiable output and objective metrics. In many mature economies, bankers and lawyers are among the best-paid professionals, even though they are often counterproductive and display parasitical business practices.

The personal interests of lawyers and financial advisors are often in conflict with the interests of their clients. Specifically, these professionals have an incentive to maximize the fees they charge. A law firm won't make much on quick mediation. A financial advisor can't make money on selling an index tracking mutual fund. The value, competitiveness, or benefit of these services is difficult to measure, partly due to direct comparisons with alternative choices being difficult to make. Furthermore, arguing counterfactuals after an event, or possible alternatives to how a scenario could have played out is mostly speculative.

Unquestionably, management is a skill that requires effectively delegating work tasks. A manager who needs to do or be personally involved in all of the important work is likely to fail by getting burnt out. Attracting people with abilities that you lack is the hallmark of a leader.

In many fields, those professionals at the top take pride in and are admired for having a bargepole Management approach. Partners in law firms, famous architects, or fashion designers are sometimes barely aware of the work that gets done, but they know how to hog all the credit and reward for its success.

However, Bargepole Management Theory distinguishes itself as a management approach in how it enables a person to actually do and say nothing or have any substantial creative input. Yet, they are able to put his or her own name to the work and achievement of others.

As a way of comparison, let's clarify the type of leader who is NOT a bargepole manager. Steve Jobs is a prime example, and he differentiated himself from bargepolers in many ways. Specifically, Jobs was the architect of a vision that he assembled a team to deliver, and he played an active role in managing that team. If Steve Jobs had instead been a bargepole manager, he would have given unspecific and generic guidelines of 'designing a product and service that is innovative and popular,' insisted on only visualizing finished products, and then taken credit for those products or services that proved successful in the marketplace.

Bargepole Management is about disassociating yourself from the creation process and thus from the accountability of outcomes and results while ultimately presenting yourself as indispensable. However, when done correctly, complete delegation with loose monitoring of employees can result in a happier workplace that can spur both creativity and maximize productivity.

A further comparison can be made to how Bargepole Theory is related to Machiavellianism, a general term for what the Oxford dictionary defines as the teachings of "cunning and duplicity to gain in statecraft or in general conduct."

Many traits of a bargepole manager are similar to those of a Machiavel. Some of the shared attributes between a Machiavel and a bargepole manager include:

▶ Hides personal convictions well

▶ Readily changes positions depending on the situation

▶ Unwilling to confess mistakes

▶ Suspicious of others' motives

▶ Does not return favors and is disingenuous in relationships

▶ Never obviously manipulative

▶ Good at identifying and attracting subjects who can easily be exploited and who are unable to retaliate

Is it possible to be both a Machiavel and a bargepole manager? The two can be difficult to tell apart, and the difference is often a matter of interpretation. But the teachings and objectives are not the same. Bargepole Theory distinguishes itself from Machiavellianism in how it teaches success without contributing any actual value to an organization. In contrast to a Machiavel, who has specific outcomes in mind with an agenda of what to achieve and how to win over others, a bargepole manager primarily focuses on how to hide lack of insight, talent, or professional ability while protecting his or her position. Inequalities are created through organizational structures in order to evade objective comparisons and evaluation of his or her work and contribution.

Naturally, bargepolers often want to perceive themselves as being Machiavels. To an extent, they are Machiavels in how many of the techniques and outcomes are similar. Indeed, the metaphor of a Machiavel being a chess master who has a strategy where he plans a large number of moves ahead is applicable. At the same time, a bargepoler is the expert who develops his or her game around sacrificing all pieces for the sake of protecting the King.

THE RELATIONSHIP TO PETER'S PRINCIPLE

Many people mistake Bargepole Management to be a version of Peter's Principle, which suggests that people get promoted until they reach their 'position of incompetence.' However, the whole concept of Bargepole Theory is to be promoted without merit.

At the same time, Peter's Principle can apply to bargepolers in that bargepolers often reach a position where they are unable, or unlikely, to further maximize their rewards with minimal input; they are also unlikely to maximize their rewards at lower risks for getting exposed.

This situation is symptomatic for many organizations where Bargepoling is rife. A large proportion of both bargepolers and firewalls have reached positions and levels of remuneration packages that they would probably be unable to get somewhere else. Job security in the form of a Patron shielding them from scrutiny is sufficient motivation for them to remain in their current job. This setup works well, especially when the jimpees on the ground are strongly motivated, creative, and deliver positive results.

CHAPTER SUMMARY

Bargepole Management Theory is best applied in an organization where rewards can be disconnected from and are not based on any actual contribution toward measurable results. Instead, rewards are based on emotional considerations of the perceived value of an individual's contribution.

The improvement of any actual performance or measurable contribution of either the individual or the organization is not the aim of Bargepoling. As such, Bargepole Management Theory principally contradicts most conventional business strategies and management theories. That being said, practically all management books target individuals that are, in fact, looking for ways to maximize rewards to exceed their potential. This is usually accomplished through methods of obscuring what is actually contributed to their organization from any real or measurable value.

The following joke that is taken from the vulgar world of finance, and made the rounds on the Internet, describes the warped form of American corporatism that Enron and the sub-prime mortgage crisis of 2008 represented.

"You have two cows. You sell three of them to your publicly listed company, using letters of credit opened by your brother-in-law at the bank, and then execute a debt/equity swap with an associated general offer so that you get all four cows back with a tax exemption for five cows. The milk rights of the six cows are transferred via an intermediary to a Cayman Island company secretly owned by the majority shareholder who sells the rights to all seven cows back to your listed company. The annual report says the company owns eight cows with an option on one more. No balance sheet is provided with the release. The public buys your bull."

This joke can also describe Bargepole Management because it obscures the fact that there is no real underlying value in what is being sold. However, the ability to sell nothing as something of premium value is not that easy.

Astute readers will argue that 'all' management literature can be techniques for Bargepoling. Examples include defining KPIs, monitoring and reporting, benchmarking, outsourcing, market diversification, and using CRM systems. Other literature includes generic talk about strategizing, market segmentation, and the need to 'set up processes.' These concepts are all useful diversion tactics and tools that a bargepole manager has at his or her disposal. The purpose of a bargepole manager is to hide his or her inability or unwillingness to take any meaningful decisions or assume any direct accountability for creating a competitive product or service.

Bargepole Management Theory can be seen as a refined version of modern management literature that unveils the real underlying motives for the readers of these books. First, these readers desire maximum benefits and rewards, irrespective and decoupled from measurable skills. Second, they want their performance or contribution to the organization to be perceived as invaluable. At the same time, they want no specific decisions to be traced back to them. The ultimate motive is to secure excessive compensation. By directly addressing what the motives are it is easier for the reader to understand how they are best accomplished.

Now that you understand the concept of bargepole management, before you stand any chance of practicing it in real life, you must adopt the psyche of a bargepoler. The following chapter describes the psychology of bargepole management.

Bargepole Management

CHAPTER 2

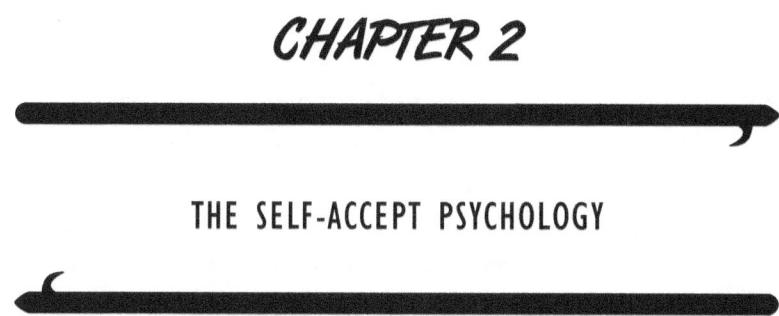

THE SELF-ACCEPT PSYCHOLOGY

'...we need to appreciate those imperfections that benefit us, recognize the ones we would like to overcome, and design the world around us in a way that takes advantage of our incredible abilities while overcoming some of our limitations.'
—Dan Ariely

The first step toward working less but achieving more is to adopt the mindset and psychology of Bargepole Management. This adoption requires two key elements. First, you must have an astute awareness of your own limitations in terms of knowledge and competence, and second, you must possess a good understanding of the personal weaknesses of colleagues competing for positions in the hierarchy of your organization.

To further clarify the first element, Bargepole Management is not about being the best or even being particularly adept; rather, it simply entails being seen as the best among those with whom you are being compared. This principle is the crux of Bargepole Management—a 'self-accept' approach that recognizes and is self-aware of personal flaws and limitations.

This requires strict discipline in order to be consistent and restrictive in personal presentation. It also requires that you not draw attention to your weaknesses; you must never put yourself in situations where you are forced to reveal them.

The second element is equally important whereby you exploit the social weaknesses of your colleagues in order to expose their lack of skill or expertise. Their weaknesses then become a central part of their professional identity in the work environment. As a result, the path is cleared for you to shine as the superior employee without your new prestige having any basis in fact.

The ultimate enabler for becoming a bargepoler is differentiation and being branded as the most complete and well-rounded person in the organization. You must outmaneuver anyone who can threaten your position by being perceived as more valuable. Likewise, you must outmaneuver anyone who can otherwise bring any attention to your flaws. You are selling a story about yourself. This approach is not about being the best; instead, it is about managing and psyching out your competition.

Whether you are employed by a small corporation or an industrial giant, and regardless of your position in a hierarchy, the concept of Bargepoling remains the same. It even applies to your social life and attracting romantic partners. Few people can rely on simply being the best looking, the most charming, or the most accomplished. Rather, success in seducing a romantic partner is about circumstances and contextualization. Your personal presentation is critical, but how and who you are allowing yourself to be compared with is most important. As an example, for a person who is rather 'average' in their native country is better served romantically if they move to a place where there is less competition or where their features are deemed exotic and attractive.

COUNTER-POSITIVE THINKING

Positive thinking is more prevalent among unskilled people than among highly skilled people. Yet, those lacking an awareness of their deficiency of talent are often found to be more productive and successful than skilled people because skilled people are restrained by an accurate understanding of their limitations. This phenomenon is referred to as the Dunning-Kruger effect.

Therefore, positive thinking can be an advantage in terms of productivity and personal happiness. It's good to have self-confidence and self-esteem. However, it is also good to know how and when self-awareness is useful. To put it baldly, resist the temptation of falling too deeply in love with your creation, it might just be shit. Having this rare insight and awareness can give you a surprisingly valuable edge over others. You see, positive thinking is ultimately a delusion among "suckers" and a tool that enables bargepole managers to exploit them.

An example is how companies recruit sales staff by only citing On Target Earnings (OTE). These companies may reveal how much the top sales representative made last month and point at the Porsche in the parking lot. 'Suckers' question the 'zero' basic salary and why commissions only kick in after reaching a very high threshold on sales. However, 'suckers' also accept the answer that this only concerns underperformers; since they are not underperformers, they too will soon be able to afford high-end sports cars.

This attitude among those people who don't recognize their own limitations is a blatant example of how a bargepoler is able to exploit a person who is suffering from the Dunning-Kruger effect. I call the approach Counter-positive Thinking. A detailed outline for how to adopt this mindset and approach is included in the appendix.

ASSOCIATING WITH SUCCESS AND DISASSOCIATING FROM FAILURE

Remember the kid in school who never bothered to play defense in soccer? By merely waiting around near the goalpost to be the first to run up and congratulate the scorer he looked like he was part of the overall effort. Dodgeball is another great example where the best and most capable players near the front line get eliminated long before the wimps hiding in the back.

This same childhood mentality and strategy is found in the adult world of corporate environments. The wimp in the back of the Dodgeball game is very likely the same guy who is now presenting those reports and taking credit for your work. Of course, in the grown-up world, there is a need to show some restraint and avoid excessive self-congratulations.

In order to maximize your remuneration in an organization, the extent of your contribution must be impossible to accurately gauge in practical or monetary terms. Placing yourself in a position where your contribution is not questioned is key. When done right, it is difficult to spot, but it can be identified by the fact that no failure can ever be traced back to the bargepoler. It is impossible for anyone to know what decisions they took or even any influence that they wielded. Corporations stigmatize mistakes to the degree that inaction and indecisiveness gets seen more as signs of sound leadership than the ability to plan and implement creative initiatives.

An effective bargepole manager is able to avoid any personal risk of being associated with failure as a result of misjudgment. Thus, even if a bargepoler is highly creative, they must refrain from laying claim to any original ideas, even if they genuinely owned them. A bargepoler will avoid the topic of what they did or didn't do altogether. Instead, it is important to project the conviction that it was only possible because the bargepoler made it possible. For similar reasons, bargepole managers avoid direct involvement in the practical delivery of a product or service being sold.

BARGEPOLE COMPETENCE

Competence is measured by the ability to derive optimal utility from employed resources at the highest possible rate of return. In contrast, incompetence is lacking awareness, both of what is needed to succeed in the first place, as well as being able to predict realistic outcomes.

Great bargepolers are similar to 'essentialists' as described by Greg Mckeown in his book Essentialism: the Disciplined Pursuit of Less. Both focus exclusively on activities where their contribution is maximised and they only get involved where they can make a positive impact! Their ethos is the same as the Hippocratic oath to first do no harm.

Being a competent bargepoler is largely about having awareness of your limitations and when and in what areas to surrender to the judgment of other people. It is here that the advantages of bargepoling are particularly clear. Faced with a situation where your judgment or interpretation of the information available is likely no better than anyone else's, there is no risk premium for supporting one view or action over another. The art of bargepoling here is about having others stake their names and reputations in the process of figuring out how to best match resources with possible opportunities considered.

There are many explanations for when professionals fail to bargepole efficiently and get exposed as incompetent. One of the more common reasons is how succeeding and following a streak of favorable outcomes from making the right judgments can turn into a disease. Under such circumstances, even the best and most competent leaders can be seduced into underestimating their competitors and overestimating both their own judgment and capacity of the resources available to them. This often plays a part in explaining the correlation seen in how complete failure often occurs shortly after an organization reaches the pinnacle of achievement.

CHAPTER 3

THE ECONOMIC PRINCIPLES OF BARGEPOLE THEORY

'Half the work that is done in the world is to make things appear what they are not.'
—E.R. Beadle

Before exploring the detailed methods of Bargepoling, this chapter provides a brief overview of the traditional management theories and the conventional economic models that make Bargepole Theory viable. In other words, these theories/models make it possible for an individual to act in a role and manipulate organizations while hiding a lack of professional expertise and leadership skills.

Bargepole Theory is relatable to familiar concepts like those found in Philip Kotler's Principles of Marketing and Michael Porter's Competitive Advantage.

Specifically, Kotler explains how a company can compete by being the first or one of the first players to enter a market or niche. He then explains how a company can successfully establish barriers to entry and/or mobility for competitors. Michael Porter describes how a company can move up the value chain by avoiding commodity-type support services and production. Instead, Porter suggests that a company focus on value-added activities in order to offer higher margins.

Bargepole Theory follows the same reasoning by demonstrating how individuals act as economic agents within an organization. Similar to the principles of Kotler and Porter, Bargepole Theory describes how a lucrative market is first identified for entry at an early stage to secure a position. Thereafter, suppressing and outmaneuvering internal competition (e.g., existing and potential colleagues) becomes the central objective.

Reducing transparency is arguably the most effective strategy for protecting market territory and maintaining high margins. Consider how credit card companies or mobile phone operators deliberately create confusion as to how charges are levied and thereby make it difficult to compare prices. Similarly, pharmaceutical companies spend more on marketing to influence the perception of their products than they spend on research and development for new drugs.

The focus shifts from transparency and allowing customers to make informed decisions based on objective comparisons between often identical products and services to reducing transparency, distorting market competitiveness, and winning customers by creating emotional bonds with their brands.

How these market strategies are deployed in the corporate world is well covered in economic theory. What Bargepole Theory adds to the mix is a layer of psychology that shows how the same unfair advantages of defusing competition and getting priced at a premium is achievable through the many social interactions that build a person's career.

REFUGE IN GENERALITY

We live in a time and age where the general trend is not to express any opinion that may be viewed as controversial. By only communicating what is already broadly agreed upon, we don't contribute any information or ideas of value. Dressing up general knowledge and neutral value statements as original thought is so common and popular because there is no benefit in expressing any opinion that can cause disagreements in personal relationships. By communicating clearly on matters, we reveal our thinking and position, which exposes us to the risks of being proven wrong and being put on the defensive.

A leader that rarely faces criticism or discontent over his or her decisions is not likely to be a good leader; rather, the lack of criticism is more likely an indication that no real decisions are being made. Bargepole Theory relies on the skill of maintaining indecision and non-position on critical matters without being seen as doing so. This technique is a way of minimizing risk and accountability.

THE ADVANTAGE OF FOLLOWING TRENDS

'It must be considered that there is nothing more difficult to carry out, nor more doubtful of success, nor more dangerous to handle, than to initiate a new order of things.'
—Niccolò Machiavelli

The impact of individuals and their singular decisions on the outcomes of a company's operations is usually overestimated. Most outcomes are determined by events and trends that are entirely beyond any one person's control. When a company fails, it is more often because the business model was fundamentally flawed rather than the result of any decision or non-decision on the part of the leader who is formally responsible.

Similar to the role of a soccer coach, what can be done from the sidelines once the game begins is limited. Yet, the ability to uphold the illusion of control and direction is a significant part of what is seen as leadership.

A bargepole manager knows that if their actual influence or contribution is impossible to measure objectively, it is more important to ensure that their is valued on emotional grounds, ideally being viewed as indispensable to the organization regardless of results. This does not detract from the need for and value of a soccer coach's skill in assembling the best-suited players. They must orchestrate the ideal circumstances, whereby the players' complementary strengths result in the best possible performance.

The approach can be understood through economist Herb Simon's Behavioral Model of Rational Choice, which argues that copying is the best strategy. It is impossible to correctly evaluate the actual costs and benefits of a certain decision with endless unknown factors to consider. The outcomes are largely inevitable according to the overriding trends in the marketplace as dictated by the collective behavior of the market players. The idea is that once something becomes a little more popular, a feedback mechanism causes positive linking. Identifying these early on and getting a 'first-follower' advantage is easier than achieving a genuine 'first-mover' advantage.

In fact, one can even argue for a first-mover disadvantage. There is no shortage of examples of pioneers being the first to introduce revolutionary innovations that would change the world only to have others profit from them while they themselves went bankrupt. Examples include the 15th-century printing press and its inventor Johannes Gutenberg, the handheld cellphones introduced by Motorola, the Netscape web-browser and the Napster file sharing software.

HEDGE FUND AND BRAND MANAGER

For an individual or group to decouple their compensation incentives from both demonstrable economic returns, as well as the interests of the company shareholders, involves skills of image control similar to a branding expert. At the same time, managing risk exposure and maximizing upside potential is comparable with a fund manager who is also able to achieve success without having any actual understanding of the industries being invested in.

Bargepole Management is about disassociating yourself from direct exposure to the creation process of a product or service in order to:

1. *Skirt accountability of all shortcomings*

By assuming responsibility for delivery of a product or service or getting involved directly in resolving a problem, your limited expertise and professional capabilities are at risk of getting exposed.

2. *Decouple the value of your work from any actual or measurable economic result or operational outcome*

When your work contribution is directly linked to an outcome, the actual value of your work can be measured. Insufficient bargepoling skills put you in this vulnerable position where you must constantly justify keeping your job. This second aspect and function of Bargepoling is about upholding the illusion that you are indispensable to an organization and should therefore be compensated accordingly, irrespective of the organization's actual performance and output.

The Bargepole Management approach is comparable to being a mix of both a hedge fund manager and a brand manager. The similarity to a hedge fund manager is in how the skill of investing strategically pertains to limiting risk exposure and downside potential. It accomplishes this limitation of risk by not being fully invested or vulnerable to any outcome or movement in the marketplace. This outcome is achieved by spreading your bets through hedging and diversification while also maximizing the upside potential by means of leverage techniques.

A bargepole manager can systematically deploy numerous projects where his or her exposure to accountability is minimized through the firewalls and safety valves created in the form of fall guys. These fall guys, also known as firewalls, are put in place to stop the bargepoler from being directly implicated in the risks taken. Meanwhile, they will have the skill to claim the credit and rewards for the successful gambles that they have green lighted.

Concurrently, with the skill of maximizing the risk premium like a hedge fund manager, the ability to brand and create a valuable image is equally important for moving up the value chain and distancing yourself from direct involvement in any work being completed.

The objective of Bargepole Management Theory can be explained as moving up the value chain by simply engaging in branding and licensing while all operational activities like production, design, development, distribution, logistics, and support functions are unloaded onto other stakeholders along with the associated expense and risk.

GETTING PRICED LIKE A LUXURY BRAND

You can compare the approach of decoupling your professional role from measurable value creation to how branded goods are priced and sold. To a greater degree, psychological projections of value determine their pricing. Pricing has nothing to do with cost of production or functional value of the product. Price has become an indicator of value and not the other way around. As such, sales, marketing, and brand building habitually command a price for a product that is more than it is actually worth.

Studies have shown that the performance of salespeople within a single company, selling identical products to the same client stock, often varies by as much as a factor of three. In many industries, the value generated is equal to the value that is projected. The work is merely about creating values that may not exist. This is only possible to do if you are able to present a market offering that cannot be compared objectively to that of a competitor; otherwise, the price can be calculated on the basis of tangible metrics.

This same logic applies to how individuals manage to project their value in an organization, and this is the aim, purpose, and reward of succeeding as a bargepole manager.

When you look at any group of employees, their pay will be based primarily on their work being measured on the basis of the following three tiers:

► Time
► Productivity that is measurable in output or results
► Perceived value to an organization and/or the emotional attachment to the person(s) determining position and salary

The third tier is the Holy Grail. It is difficult to get there, and it is even more difficult to stay there. The following chapters will discuss how the journey of getting there is about a mindset more than anything else.

Bargepole Management

CHAPTER 4

A HOW-TO GUIDE: IMPLEMENTING THE BARGEPOLE STRATEGY

The man who makes no mistakes does not usually make anything.

—Edward Phelps

While it may seem obvious and simple to understand how bargepolers operate, it is not! Thus far you have only scratched the surface. This book will now teach you the intricate method to the madness of successfully implementing the strategies.

This how-to guide covers the seven key aims of bargepoling:

► Identifying and accessing bargepole-conducive work environments.

► Projecting an image of being critically important and beyond reproach.

► Crafting the bargepole hierarchy of power patrons, firewalls, and jimpees.

► Creating power distances and maintaining a lack of transparency.

► Establishing false meritocracies.

► Detaching the value of your work contribution from quantifiable measurement.

► Being compensated based on emotionally perceived value.

These seven key aims are all interconnected and are further broken down into the following three groups of bargepole enablers:

1. Identifying and accessing a work environment that is conducive to bargepole management.

2. Social engineering and maneuvering of the organizational environment.

3. Interpersonal social skills and manipulation.

First we'll explain the three enablers from the perspective of an individual acting within an organization and outline the steps required to succeed. Then we'll move beyond the individual and apply the enablers to companies competing in the marketplace. Finally we'll analyze the principles of bargepole theory from a macro perspective on the scale of corporate and national governance.

THE THREE BARGEPOLE ENGABLERS

Bargepole enabler one: identifying and accessing work environments conducive to bargepole management.

Markets, industries, or sectors with little competition, performance benchmarks, or reliability of information are conducive to bargepoling. Immature industries and growth markets tend to be fertile ground. Also, jobs that are not clearly correlated with performance—such as in government sectors, NGOs, and industries protected by monopolies and rewards—are ideal for bargepoling.

Bargepole enabler two: social engineering and maneuvering of the organizational environment

An environment that is conducive to bargepoling, once created, must always be maintained in order to make long-term bargepoling possible. To do so we use a series of different methods, including creating massive power differentials between layers in hierarchies; restricting transparency; and projecting false meritocracies, where staff is motivated by carrot dangling. In other words, rewards appear to be based on work performance, skill, and contribution toward results. Maintaining a high turnover of junior staff along with an influx of new, gullible staff is an important component of upholding the stability of bargepole environments.

Bargepole enabler three: interpersonal social skills and manipulation

This category involves securing a hierarchical position by suppressing the internal competition from your colleagues. Ideally you make your colleagues promote your interests as the bargepoler in the mistaken belief that it is benefiting them.

An overriding approach bargepolers rely on are the 'Master Suppression Techniques', a framework for establishing dominance and sideline colleagues. These can often be carried out with such finesse that they go unnoticed. For instance, a bargepoler may appear helpful by putting his hand on your shoulder and explain basic steps of a procedure you are familiar with, give broadly known background information, or congratulate your work on a simple and insignificant task. This is not out of kindness or to show support but to limit your perceived standing and potential to the other members in the organization. Four of the main Master Suppression Techniques include ridicule, withholding information, belittling and shaming.

MASTERING BARGEPOLE ENABLER I

Identifying and accessing work environments conducive to Bargepole Management

STEP I — IDENTIFYING BARGEPOLE CONDUCIVE ENVIRONMENTS

Indeed, certain industries in specific geographical markets are better suited than others for Bargepoling. Therefore, choosing where to bargepole is one of the first and most important steps. In short, the most ideal circumstance for being a successful bargepole manager is where the cause and effect of decisions is unclear and where both the pricing as well as the delivery of the product or service is primarily based on intangible factors. For example, emerging markets and industries that are immature and possess a shortage of readily available information and benchmarks for professional performance are ideal circumstances for Bargepoling.

Two Examples of Bargepole Conducive Environments:

A company or organization that is active in a market or industry where the product and service is highly intangible

Ideal market or industry candidates for Bargepoling include legal services, financial services, media, telecom, marketing, and hospitality. However, the most suitable sectors for Bargepoling are by far government, NGOs or associations.

Bargepoling is more challenging in mature industries with an established history of performance or otherwise very clear expectations of output and profitability. For example, mature sectors such as manufacturing, farming, food processing, forestry, and traditional healthcare services are less ideal for bargepole managers because benchmarks for performance are clear, and perceptions are not easily skewed. In essence, these are sectors where soft skills with intangible value don't offer a premium over verifiable ability to do a job that has a measurable result. The key to being a bargepole manager is the opportunity to obscure connections between cause and effect that can be traced to specific decisions and the impact of those decisions in results.

Immature business sector and/or emerging market

In markets where benchmarks for quality and professional performance have yet to be established, the premium of simply being an actor that is acting in a role is maximized. Here, soft social skills that build alliances, project credibility, and avoid being questioned on actual skills, competence, or educational background are essential.

TRAITS AND SYMPTOMS OF BARGEPOLE-PRONE ORGANIZATIONS

Identifying organizations that are prone to Bargepoling will help you recognize and understand the circumstances as well as market conditions for when Bargepoling is possible and also beneficial. It will also help you determine when a bargepoler is likely to be detrimental to a company's performance.

Organizations that are prone to Bargepoling have distinct layers in their hierarchy. Yet almost everyone has a fancy job title such as director, regional manager, or vice president.

Generally, companies displaying extensive bargepole traits in their organization are in industry sectors where sales and marketing activities as well as general appearances offer the best return on utilized time and resources. Their product or service quality is difficult to gauge and price as it is not based on any tangible value that can be measured according to objectively comparable metrics.

Typical Traits of Bargepole Prone Organizations:

▶ Excessive premiums on avoiding blame for failure

▶ Acting in self-interest that is asymmetrical to the interests of the organization

▶ Lack of honesty, feedback, or input on weaknesses of plans and strategies

▶ Strong focus on job titles and perks that show position in hierarchy

▶ Origin and ultimate accountability for decisions is unclear

▶ Employees generally think they are smarter than everyone else yet refrain from airing opinions

▶ The normal tone for communication is in a contrived voice that expresses authority, sucking up, feigned interest, or false enthusiasm

To identify and understand a bargepole-prone organization, it is helpful to examine the traits of organizations that are NOT bargepole-prone. These are the organizations that have low power distances between hierarchical layers, and they are often referred to as having flat organization structures. Open communication and pragmatic approaches to solving problems are encouraged, which make these environments less conducive to Bargepoling.

Typical Traits of Non-Bargepole Prone Organizations:

▶ Sense of purpose and a common identity

▶ Employees are intrinsically driven to deliver on clear and common goals

▶ Encouragement of objective criticism on weaknesses in strategies, processes, and business plans

▶ Disagreements are not cause for emotional trauma and result in positive feedback loops being created

STEP 2 – GAINING ACCESS TO BARGEPOLE CONDUCIVE ENVIRONMENTS

There is no question that many, if not most, people who were afforded an opportunity to become bargepolers did so as a consequence of sheer luck. Nonetheless, luck had nothing to do with their ability to seize the opportunity and capitalize on it over the long term.

Bargepolers have the good sense and nerve to take advantage of such opportunities that arise from being in the right time and place. This involves having the talent to read people and situations. You must deliberately frame these encounters into contexts that support your agenda. The ability to manipulate key colleagues to forward your cause by making them think that this promotes their own interests is the core foundation for becoming a bargepoler.

This book cannot teach you how to place yourself in the right time and place with the right people to open the doors to a bargepole position. There is no explicit recipe or step-by-step guide for this component.

Obtaining a bargepole position often requires a mix of several strategies in order to gain the trust of senior managers. It is also to undercut colleagues who are competing to be seen in a favorable light. Because these tactics are highly personal in nature, the style and approach varies significantly depending on individual circumstances and personalities. Pure office politics, or the study of psychological dispositions of managers, office personalities, and workers' behavior, is not within the realm of Bargepole Management.

This section will cover numerous scenarios and behaviors that are typically found in the ascendance of bargepolers, such as outmaneuvering colleagues or winning the favor of the Patrons.

The most common trait and success factor for bargepole managers is coming across as authentic. When acting with selfish agendas, a person who makes such an agenda less obvious is far likelier to succeed. A general rule of thumb is to strongly rely on one Power Patron rather than several; this is the better and safer strategy. Your loyalties and usefulness to this person must be seen as complete and unquestionable. This principle is no different than a man who has a high tolerance for a lover as long as basic loyalty is not broken.

The following is an outline of typical scenarios that can help to identify windows of opportunity to access a bargepole position.

Scenario & Strategy 1: Early Entry in a Company or New Division to Secure Position

One of the most important elements, which can be treated as a first step in becoming a bargepoler, is finding an untapped niche in the market or company where you can create and defend a fiefdom.

A common example is found in fast-growing companies among IT managers. A company's first IT employee, who started out as a temp and was responsible for a handful of computers, managed to claw his way to the top of the pile. Even when the company grew to hundreds or thousands of employees and the true skill or knowledge was far out of his competence level, he remained on top. Naturally, it does help if he was able to point to at least some concrete examples of delivering results at some stage.

Other examples include industries in less attractive fields or new geographic locations that don't attract top talent or serious competition. These are good places to embark on a journey of Bargepoling.

Scenario & Strategy 2: Projecting a Persona in Possession of Critical Contacts and Influence

A typical strategy for jokers and wannabe bargepolers is to exaggerate personal influence over others to project themselves as more influential and powerful than is actually the case.

While this practice is very common, it can also easily backfire if a person is exposed for not having the connections and friends claimed. From the start, Bargepoling is about perceived value instead of actual value or any value that can be measured, compared, or verified. Constant awareness of this principle is paramount.

Scenario & Strategy 3: Power Connection

Conventional forms of sucking up, by means of ass kissing and flattery, are not often effective for obtaining a bargepole position. However, more refined and subtle forms of sucking up do play a part, but these techniques are used in building the friendship connection.

An obvious example is the son who has a direct line to the owner (his father) of the company. Other examples include when there is a special connection due to shared ethnicity, religious beliefs, or alma mater. Even so, the ability to leverage the value of these connections involves an element of tactfully sucking up.

The value of perceived friendship tends to be based on people having a higher degree of trust based on likeability and assumed similarities in backgrounds or shared views as well as ways of reasoning. Even without any direct or concrete similarities, a socially astute person that is in tune with other people is able to convincingly play on this concept to his or her advantage. In other words, "People don't like you for who you are but for how you make them feel about themselves."

These power connections are the basis for how a con man operates. However, the discussion about how psychopaths can be successful in corporate politics is a separate subject, and it is only tangentially related to the art of bargepole management.

Scenario & Strategy 4: Silent Blackmail and Interdependence

Unlike a form of traditional blackmail that includes direct threats, this silent blackmail strategy is about obtaining and maintaining the right opportunities to gain incriminating knowledge or compromising information. Specifically, this strategy can strengthen your position by making others vulnerable.

This strategy can also put those who influence or grant access to power (Patrons) in a position where an unspoken power balance is maintained. This feat is accomplished by keeping hidden information from being used against them. The strategy of blackmail is also effective in defusing threats from colleagues that are competing for favor from the same Patrons in an organization, granting them influential positions.

Scenario & Strategy 5: Tokenism

The most obvious bargepole positions involve scenarios of tokenism. This is when a blatant disconnect appears between a person's performance and merit on the one side with reward and hierarchical position on the other but gets accepted in the name of tolerance and equality.

There are various degrees of this Tokenism scenario, and there is no shortage of examples to illustrate how it is practiced. However, a common example is the promotion and defense of a barely qualified candidate who is of a certain perceived minority or discriminated against group, in fear of being seen as sexist, racist, homophobic, or otherwise intolerant.

Success by playing the 'token card' is not as simple as merely belonging to a group and claiming special treatment. Instead, this strategy is related to the 'Power Connection' strategy. The rules of engagement for Bargepoling still apply if you are both incompetent and belong to a certain group or ethnicity that is perceived to be in need of special treatment. Succeeding here makes it even more important to not get compared on performance.

The advantages of Tokenism are that it offers access, and it then becomes a tool to continuously avoid getting questioned on contribution or value. However, when you pursue Tokenism as a strategy, the constant battle you will face is projecting such an image of value above reproach while not being accused of Tokenism by your colleagues.

MASTERING BARGEPOLE ENABLER TWO:

SOCIAL ENGINEERING IN THE ORGANIZATIONAL ENVIRONMENT

Before discussing the individual behavior behind mastering bargepole techniques, the organizational structure and culture required for Bargepoling will first be explained in further detail. The control of communication between parties makes it possible to influence what, in fact, gets communicated.

The influence of information is central for remaining in a bargepole position. Specifically, you must influence how such information is made available, its recipients, and how it is interpreted. As a bargepoler, you must project value and obscure the reality that you have no actual function or purpose. This section outlines how to structure an organization and design a hierarchy so that social engineering of this nature is possible in the work environment.

CRAFTING THE FOUR-LAYER BARGEPOLE HIERARCHY

SELECTING A LINE-UP OF PATRONS, FIREWALLS AND JIMPEES

Securing a Power Patron

The value of bargepolers may be unseen and unrelated to their contribution to the results of the organization. Yet, bargepolers will need to somehow convince a Patron to obtain a position of power and privilege. To achieve this step, the aspiring bargepoler must present the Patron with some form of value proposition.

While it may seem that bargepolers are of no practical value to the performance of an organization, the value that they offer their Patrons often comes in the form of some kind of protection. This protection may include creating and upholding artificial power, addressing imbalances between layers of the hierarchy, or steering uncomfortable questions away from them.

Selecting Firewalls

The most important decisions you will make as a successful bargepole manager are choosing your 'henchmen' or firewalls. This first layer of defense for a bargepoler is a line-up of personnel who serve as firewalls against direct accountability for the bargepoler. In other words, these firewalls protect the bargepoler from blame.

Specifically, the function of firewalls is to explain and to credibly take on blame so that the bargepoler is always seen in a positive light. In no small part, firewalls must take unpopular decisions and deliver them downward while accepting accountability for such decisions. If necessary, a firewall must even take a fall for the bargepoler. As a result, the ideal firewall is someone who is predictably loyal and does not delude themselves into thinking that they can rise above the bargepoler to whom they answer.

Firewalls also serve as a buffer between the bargepoler and the frontline tier of jimpees. These are the individuals who are doing the practical work of developing, producing, and delivering the products and services. Likewise, firewalls stand tall as barriers that ensure minimal communication between the bargepoler and the jimpees. These barriers prevent the bargepoler from getting asked to become involved or being implicated in whatever problems may arise. In the case of legal action, it is further beneficial to be able to claim ignorance.

Firewalls thrive on the feeling of being in charge; they are often a little sadistic as well. This characteristic comes in handy when recruiting jimpees. Firewalls present jimpee job applicants with a basic salary, which is practically nothing, and they make this compensation sound like a good deal. Additionally, they overwhelm jimpee applicants with empty promises that tend to include acronyms such as OTE (On Target Earnings) and opportunities for fast-tracked career progression.

SOURCING THE JIMPEES (USEFUL IDIOT WORKERS)

You may have gathered that jimpees are those employees in the organization who do what they are told. The ideal jimpee is highly dependent on his or her salary, afraid of losing his or her job, and is hungry, if not desperate, to prove themselves. Jimpees are therefore easy to control, and they are also easy to manipulate through a simple pat on the back. Vague promises of lavish rewards that are supposedly linked to their loyalty and performance can easily keep them productive and effective for at least one year.

Unlike the firewalls, line managers, or directors to whom they report, jimpees think that the sky is the limit, and they believe that they might one day be the CEO of the company. They are encouraged in this delusion in the same way that they are made to believe that their pay is based on performance.

Jimpees are never paid enough for them to feel their current positions are long-term career options. Low wages, along with disappointment over salary increases, bonuses, or promotions that never materialize, ensure that a high turnover of jimpee staff occurs naturally. If jimpees don't quit of their own volition, pressure of increased targets, or unmanageable workloads are placed on them to eventually reach the point that it becomes untenable to stay on the job.

The overall idea is that new jimpees cycle through the organization with fresh energy. They are blissfully ignorant about the missing carrot at the end of the stick and lack of career progression opportunities. A high turnover of jimpee staff is also important to serve as a safety valve in case one of the jimpees learns too much or otherwise becomes a threat to any significant bargepoler in the organization.

CASE STUDY: INDIA AS A BRITISH COLONY

THE FUNCTION OF FIREWALLS AND JIMPEES IN THE BARGEPOLE HIERARCHY

As a British colony, India had less than 1,000 British bargepoler that ran the colony. Much of their efficiency can be explained by how they perfected the Bargepole Hierarchical Structure with its function of firewalls and jimpees. The case study of India as a British colony is used here to demonstrate how the same mechanisms apply and can benefit modern organizations but in a new guise.

Most colonial empires were built on the concept of divide and conquer while letting others fight the battles. The fundamental strategies of bargepole management are based on this same concept, but not in the way that most might assume.

The Indian colonial subjects did not believe that they were comparable with the British bargepolers. No matter how well these Indians learned to fake their British accents, they were not allowed to delude themselves into thinking that they could, or even should, become part of the British Bargepoling class. This idea was just as unlikely as the British Bargepole Class being encouraged to intermarry with their colonial subjects.

Today, this same mentality can be seen in a bargepoler's second-in-command. This firewall may have significant personal deficiencies that they realize would disavow them from moving above their current role as a firewall or prevent them from obtaining a similar position elsewhere. This individual often lacks academic degrees to lean on, is slightly socially awkward, and may even have some form of a physical handicap or a criminal record that limits his or her ability to gain promotion. It may appear that they overcame such handicaps to land in their current position. Yet, these handicaps are typically assets for such firewall positions.

In turn, just like the Indians in the British colony, the ideal firewall does not delude themselves into thinking that they can rise above the bargepoler to whom they answer. If the firewall does indicate such thoughts, the bargepoler should remove this firewall or remind them of the aforementioned personal deficiencies in order to create self-doubt in the firewall.

Firewalls will mostly be content with their station and understand the function they are getting paid to serve. Yet, they often overestimate the extent that their loyalty will be reciprocated in times of need. This case is often seen when banks collapse or when authorities prosecute illegal business practices.

APPLYING COLONIAL STRATEGIES IN MODERN ORGANIZATIONS

The central lesson in how the British ran their colonies by applying bargepole principles is found in the structure of their organization with firewalls and jimpees. Specifically, the colonies had easily identifiable demarcations to separate layers into hierarchies such as nationality, race, language, religion, class, and caste. While such demarcation lines are no longer as clear cut, the aim of Bargepoling is nonetheless to replicate the layers in a hierarchy so that the organization functions the same way with the bargepoler, firewalls, and jimpees.

In order to successfully replicate the British colonial environment for effective Bargepoling, an organization must be created where there is no clear overview of information and accountability. Highly diverse expat environments are ideal as the bargepoler is able to loosely define acceptable expectations in terms of behavior and workload. However, these expectations are not precisely clear because agreed-upon benchmarks have not been established. This ambiguity is not due to how things are discussed; instead, it depends on what it is possible to keep out of the discussion altogether.

ESTABLISHING AND UPHOLDING FALSE MERITOCRACIES

In bargepole organizations, perception between members of the separate layers in a hierarchy differs radically in regard to how they view the purpose and functions of different members in an organization. This is how bargepole organizations differentiate from other organizations that display a similar setup of hierarchical layers.

In turn, modern bargepole hierarchies differentiate from hierarchies of colonial times in how jimpees are incentivized and controlled. Obviously, outright slave labor is no longer an available option, so it has been replaced by establishing False Meritocracies.

False Meritocracy is the tool used to convince the frontline staff of jimpees that their hard work and results will be fairly rewarded and recognized. Meanwhile, the firewalls have been around long enough to understand that individual results are secondary to remuneration. Yet, they are made to overestimate how their loyalty in defending the bargepoler will be rewarded. Together, these concepts are the core of what makes it possible to uphold a bargepole organization in the long term.

Modern bargepole organizations are hinged on feeding the jimpees delusional ideas about their prospects. As a side note, it is possible that the British Empire, as well as the Soviet Empire, could have survived if they had determined how to trick the jimpees into thinking that sudden wealth was achievable by anyone. This is the winning formula that the modern day American Empire is built on.

MASTERING BARGEPOLE ENABLER THREE:

INTERPERSONAL SOCIAL SKILLS AND MANIPULATION

Step One

Communicating as a Bargepoler

Applying bargepole concepts in practice is all about controlling communication to influence perception of information.

Arguably, most problems, conflicts, and perceived crises are based on emotion rather than objective differences of opinion. As such, it is paramount to influence how information is perceived and interpreted. In short, what 'appears and feels to be important' is more important than 'what is important'.

Communicating as a bargepole manager involves avoiding partiality, making commitments, or interpreting information on any matter that is uncertain. Instead, the bargepole manager must wait for outcomes and create a revisionist narrative on what and who led to these decisions. 'Non-substance communication' is the standard operating procedure for professionals wanting to keep all options open by not offending anyone. The use of platitudes, as well as the avoidance of the use of value statements to thereby support or agree with everyone and everything, is essential until it is an advantage to change positions.

In Bargepole Theory, non-substance communication is elevated as a technique to give credence to, in hindsight, having foreseen any outcome. The epitome of this process is to say that you feel, believe, and make open-ended speculations; pontificate on the various courses of action available; and never express anything in absolutes. The name of the game is to align with everyone at the outset, ultimately side with the winner after the results, and then fire the loser. The key is avoiding being identified as having any specific belief that can be deemed as incongruent with other opinions and positions at a later stage.

Politicians are the main role models for how to maintain a non-specific and noncommittal language and demeanor. The trick is striking the perfect balance of being authoritative, balanced, and intellectual, while at the same time having the leadership traits of passion and a 'can-do' spirit. Politicians appear to never be unclear about what they want and say. This is a difficult balancing act.

Likewise, the hallmark of bargepole communication is to uphold an image whereby energy and style can be substituted for substance. At the same time, they are considered concise and to the point. When you feel that you strongly agree with a person, but you can't distinguish them expressing anything that is potentially contentious in any way, it is a good indication of this bargepole communication principle.

There is no single way to correctly communicate as a successful bargepoler. The chosen communication style and approach must align with your personality in order to be effective, natural, and consistent. Below are a few examples of the main objectives behind mastering non-substance communication. The following are indicative of being a bargepoler.

Non-Substance Communication

Managing Risk with Vague Views and Strong Reputation

"Even a fool, when he holdeth his peace, is counted wise: and he that shutteth his lips is esteemed a man of understanding."
- Proverbs 17:28

Bargepoling is a game of appearances, and when you say less than is actually necessary, you appear to be more in control. Silence makes people insecure. It is our instinct to want to make credible assumptions, interpretations, and explanations for the motivations and thoughts of those around us.

In most areas of life, the less you say, the more profound and mysterious you appear. It can be nearly impossible to get people to do what you want them to do by reasoning with them. Attempting to reason with another person is counter to the vein of Bargepoling. When you reason with another person, you make yourself available, and as a result, you put yourself on the same level as him or her. This action puts you at risk of being challenged, if for no better reason than to test the limits through a power standoff. In general, the more that is said to explain an argument or position, the less wise and confident you will seem. Lawyers have a saying; 'the side doing most of the talking is losing'.

Non-Substance Communication for Deflecting Accountability

The technique of non-substance communication is related to the philosophy of finding 'Refuge in Generality' as described by Herb Simon's Behavioral Model. By avoiding explicit decisions and refusing to reveal any clear position, the opportunity to wait and see, which tends naturally take root, is possible.

Bargepolers achieve this objective by being aware of how we listen. While schools teach reading and writing from the start, little emphasis is placed on listening skills. Bernard Ferrari, author of Power Listening, outlines interesting stereotypes of bad listening habits to avoid. He also highlights those listening habits that are worthwhile. Ironically, many of these 'bad' listening habits are often tools that enable Bargepoling. Below are a series of examples.

When difficult situations arise, a skilled bargepoler will appear to be engaged in productive dialogue, but they will never actually advance the conversation. The bargepoler is simply reiterating the same points or merely rephrasing what is already known. Typical strategies include making comments on the pros and cons of alternative courses of action or insisting on only seeing finished ideas.

A bargepoler want to seem wise and balanced by staying on the fence so as to buy time and await developments. Typical techniques for achieving this objective include nodding at the right moments to show engagement, finishing sentences to show understanding, and feigning empathy. Rarely is a person's position and argument supporting anything primarily fact-based. Therefore, it is best to avoid the risk of being resented by pointing out facts and realities. It is more effective to focus communication on controlling emotional responses rather than appealing to logic and rationality.

These techniques should be used without ever formally agreeing with anything. Instead, one should merely express a cordial comprehension to thwart any possibility of accountability. A valuable strategy for bargepolers is knowing how to frame conversations so as not to be tied down to any specific belief that one could be asked to defend or which could be highlighted as incongruent with other opinions.

For bargepolers, listening and responding to critical information risks exposing their weakness in terms of uncertainty and doubt. Bargepolers are most dangerous and counterproductive in this situation because they hold others back in times of crisis or significant market changes.

Keeping a Comfortable Distance

Success in consistently delivering credible, non-substance communication is linked closely with building a bargepole persona. This persona is easier to achieve by avoiding unnecessary risks that result from being associated with any group or person with distinguishable views. The central philosophy of the Bargepole Management approach is to keep a comfortable distance from these unnecessary risks.

Generally, a bargepoler should not cultivate close ties or loyalties to groups or individuals because they can then maintain anonymity. This anonymity is a great asset to a bargepole manager. They may have an outgoing and pleasant personality and know everyone on a first name basis, but speculation and the forming of opinions on personality is likely to lead to unwanted attention. It is better to fit into a mold while having the main thing, such as 'he's a nice guy,' spoken behind your back. It only takes one socially influential person taking issue with your personality to damage the brand reputation that you have established. In the worst case, the wrong person can be offended for no reason, causing irreparable harm.

As such, one should avoid provoking feelings of envy and jealousy in people in order to avoid inciting negative emotions. This applies to both those people above and below you in the hierarchy. In most industries and work environments, this principle dictates that it is usually not advisable to act boastfully by driving an expensive sports car or showing off an attractive girlfriend. Our natural instinct is to want to see such people fail unless we feel other rules apply to them. As a bargepoler, it is important to not overstep too early in this category unless it is safe to do so.

The difficulty is maintaining a balance of a personal image that is separated from others to avoid direct comparison while simultaneously being seen as sharing and promoting the group's interests.

STEP TWO

Awareness And Exploitation of Biases

Bargepole Theory teaches how to obscure information in order to deflect blame and to take undue credit for positive outcomes. These strategies that make Bargepole Theory work are based on fundamental theories found in conventional books on psychology. These familiar concepts include:

Confirmation Bias - This is when we accept information presented to us as valid if it supports what we already believe as being true. Likewise, we subconsciously discredit or ignore this information if we previously believed it to be untrue.

Negativity Bias – This is when strong alarmist information receives disproportionate attention, and it is seen as more relevant and urgent, possibly distracting from questioning the credibility of the source.

The Bandwagon Effect – This describes the behavior in which we suspend our critical thinking when under the impression that if a crowd subscribes to a certain belief, there must be some truth to it.

The Just-World Fallacy – This explains why people rewrite and re-interpret facts and events to support their wishful thinking. Cause and effect are not always absolute because things turn out a certain way 'for a reason' and 'good things happen to good people.' In contrast, events that are too random, unfair, or favor the bad guy over the good guy are more difficult to accept.

Variations of these biases are a modus operandi in strategies employed by you as a bargepole manager with the objective of obscuring and framing information as well as communication to your advantage.

Oversimplifying to Deflect Complexity

Social context and interactions shape our beliefs, and they are a handicap for effectively identifying and solving problems because we actively choose to disregard plain observations that are incongruent with our vested emotions. Unwittingly, people allow blinders to be put on them when they are beguiled into focusing on currently fashionable causes and having views that are seen as acceptable by the public. This natural urge can be expertly exploited by bargepolers in order to avoid and maintain distance from complex evaluation of problems and situations.

When you consider the vast amounts of information that every person consumes on a daily basis, it is fascinating to see how instinctively we are able to break down and simplify problems into black and white views. Consider the second invasion of Iraq in 2003, and reflect on how it divided the world population into two sides. Each side held on to their irrefutable facts that could not reasonably be argued against.

For instance, conversations are usually not about broadening or discovering new and complementing perspectives to one's own. No matter how complex a topic, most discussions are exercises in comparing checklists of typical views to determine the camp to which each one belongs.

In psychology, this concept is known as splitting: choosing to strongly support a simplified extreme of a complex issue while rejecting conflicting arguments. Splitting allows us to be more decisive and to avoid doubt and ambiguity.

As a bargepoler, it is critical to overcome the inhibition and be able to silently say difficult phrases to yourself: 'I am not able to do that', 'I was wrong', and 'I don't know.' The ability to state these phrases is important for a clearer and more accurate awareness than the awareness of the people around you.

The rare and difficult skill to question your own assumptions and realize that many of our beliefs are diluted into simplified components is a common weakness that Bargepole Theory teaches how to exploit. This skill involves encouraging people to make false assumptions based on seemingly moral grounds to benefit their interests and ulterior motives. A master class of this in action is Al Gore recording his presentation and slideshow mixing science and science fiction in 'An Inconvenient Truth.' How this principle is put into practice will be discussed in great detail towards the end of this book.

Overcoming the Illusory Superiority Bias

We are encouraged daily to have faith in ourselves and be unrealistically positive about our abilities, strengths, and knowledge. In one way or another, practically everyone has been conditioned to believe that they and their children have above average intelligence and skills in most areas.

The Illusory Superiority Bias or Complex goes by many different names in the study of cognitive psychology. Some of the names include above average bias, leniency error, sense of relative superiority, primus inter pares, First Among Equals, better-than-average phenomenon, and the Lake Wobegon Effect. These terms describe how we as people tend to think that we are better than is actually the case. We are all better drivers and lovers, more socially adaptable, ethical and intelligent as well as better looking, less prejudiced, and likely to live longer than the average person.

One of the more amusing examples of this is a survey of 829,000 high-school seniors where 0 percent rated themselves below average in "ability to get along with others," 60 percent rated themselves in the top 10 percent, and 25 percent rated themselves in the top 1 percent.

Many variants of the Illusory Superiority Bias serve as a self-serving bias.

It distorts our perceptual process to maintain and enhance self-esteem. The essence of this bias is our refusal to accept and consider negative feedback but instead focus on our strengths at the cost of overlooking our weaknesses. This bias can clearly be seen when we believe ourselves to be more valuable and responsible for the success of a group in which we are associated, and underestimating the value of our co-workers. This belief shields us from emotionally stressful impulses such as doubt and depression that would diminish our drive and self-confidence. Yet it comes at a great risk and disadvantage in how it skews our perception and hampers our ability to act and reason rationally.

When everyone believes that they are above average, deserve more credit over their colleagues for their contribution, and even think that they are indispensable to the team, it becomes inevitable that disagreements arise about how rewards should be divided. In fact, it could easily be argued that the entire theory of Bargepole Management caters to and exacerbates people who suffer and seek justification for their Illusory Superiority Bias. Everyone has had to suffer through long harangues from colleagues and friends who speak about their boss who is completely useless and is a total bargepoler.

Self-serving biases or delusions are stronger and more prevalent than ever because they are actively promoted as virtues and strengths. When you couple these biases with our desire to fit in socially, such as when we avoid turning down offers and requests to be polite, the result is behavior that is counter-productive and self-sabotaging at best; it is outright destructive to us at worst. Foremost, it hampers us from correctly assessing people, situations, our own abilities, and making decisions that are likely to result in the desired outcomes. As a bargepoler, it is important to have an awareness of how these handicaps influence thinking, both your own and that of those around you. This awareness allows you to avoid behaving irrationally, and it also helps you exploit colleagues who are easily manipulated due to their inferior logic.

Independent Interpretation of Information

"...the most successful man in life is the man who has the best information."
—*Benjamin Disraeli*

Despite living in an information age where the average person has attended college and consumes hours of news each day, we are more incapable than ever to apply rational and critical analysis to the information we are fed. Likewise, we are also incapable of applying and relating to our own situations.

Consider how conversations are usually not related to broadening or discovering new or complementing perspectives to one's own. No matter how complex a topic, most discussions are exercises in comparing checklists of typical views to determine the camp to which each one belongs. Our views are not shaped by any intellectual exercise of determining what we believe to be accurate and true. Instead, we choose our beliefs based on how we think it would reflect on us and define us in our social environment.

Effective Bargepoling is about distorting information to others by mixing in emotional values, morals, and peer pressure from social behavior. In other words, bargepolers manipulate others by how events are interpreted and how information is perceived.

Master bargepolers are set apart from the rest by their ability to understand that veracity and accuracy of information is not fixed, but instead it is in a constant flux. Reality is defined continuously and is dependent on perspectives that can be shaped and altered. The primary psychological requisites that make this possible, is how what is perceived to be fact or reality is an illusion in our daily lives; the perception is made up of the most popular collective biases and is largely referred to as 'public opinion' or 'politically correct' opinions.

When going beyond 'non-substance communication' to push your agenda or a certain understanding of a matter, these biases must not be contradicted. Instead, find ways to frame information and point of view in a way that it is emotionally perceived to be what the person already believes or supports.

Most 'truths' are not based on verifiable and historical facts. Instead, these 'truths' are based on what does not contradict the values and beliefs that feel good and conform to our desires. If you are unaware of this bias as a handicap of questioning facts, you are easily vulnerable to illogical arguments that are counter to your own self-interests.

Overall, people tend to be emotionally intuitive in their decision-making processes. For instance, evaluating the quality, value and price of a product or service is largely based on social experience and perceived quality. This is in contrast to objectively comparing function and worth with competing offers. People still want to believe that they have reached their decisions and conclusions based on objective consideration from information gathered. By understanding this need, the bargepoler is able to tailor how options and arguments are presented.

A rhetorical tactic that is analogous to how bargepolers filter reality is "verbal virtuosity". Thomas Sowell described this as when evidence, logic and analysis are replaced with a mix of clever phrasing, vague euphemisms, witty quotes, deceptive labeling and name-calling. As such, plain and factual observations can readily be dismissed as simplistic and those making them are portrayed as lacking in morals.

The following section outlines ways for obscuring and framing information as a tool to repackage interpretations and opinions as truths and facts. This technique is for the purpose of exploiting people in your environment.

Rewriting History

Our minds are almost incapable of allowing us to remember any instances when we were wrong. At best, we may be able to admit to having been misinformed or led astray in our thinking. This self-defense mechanism even has us creating completely false memories to reframe our mistakes so that they make sense and serve a purpose.

No one, not even the best and the brightest, is immune to false memories. Hillary Clinton claimed on numerous occasions, with apparent sincerity, that she remembered landing in Bosnia under sniper fire and running with her head down to a waiting car for cover. When footage was found of her very relaxed and peaceful arrival that day, she claimed to have misspoken. Even worse than altering memories from our past, we suffer from similar handicaps in our failure to correctly interpret our present reality. Every day, we are often unable to see plain facts, causal links, or a lack of anything that runs counter to our beliefs.

While at times we may be forced to realize that we were mistaken or misinformed, we rarely have the intellectual capacity to recognize how our thinking, our de facto cognitive abilities to reason and interpret information, may have been to blame for making completely incorrect conclusions. As a result, you should be very skeptical whenever you hear any talk about learning from past mistakes.

Making up stories to make sense of, rationalize, and justify our past mistakes is part of what makes us human. All of the bad choices we made need purpose, reason, and meaning to make our conscience bearable. This desire to feel that we are right can be even stronger than our interest for the underlying issues and decisions that are at stake.

If played correctly, possessing insight into how people are driven by emotion when interpreting not only the past but also the present situation can be very powerful. At the same time, it is also important to know how this insight can be played against you. In the context of a group, flock animal instinct can be so overpowering that it can be used to convince a person to acknowledge and believe something other than what is plainly right in front of them.

Masterful bargepolers take advantage of flock animal instinct by confusing people about their memory as well as their broad understanding of a specific matter. In the end of George Orwell's Animal Farm, Piggy implants a false memory in all the farm animals by telling how he valiantly led the uprising against the farmers along with Boxer. Despite being wholly untrue, the false memory gets accepted as truth. Most people who attempt this strategy are very clumsy, if not stupid. For example, salesmen and lawyers often put words in your mouth or twist the meaning of your previous statements. Likewise, the most common example is claiming that a promise had been made and that it must be kept.

The framing of events and information by presenting a certain understanding of it to be the overwhelmingly dominant public opinion makes it naturally become the only accepted attitude and opinion. When done convincingly, it can not only change interpretations of history (i.e. how and what events transpired), but it becomes possible to influence the perception of the present reality by what courses of action can be expected or tolerated. To paraphrase the singer Jackson Browne, while the future's there for anyone to change, sometimes it's easier to change the past.

The strategy described above is dependent on having already established significant clout to influence the consciousness of a person or group. Typically, it is not possible for most individuals acting independently. Significantly establishing or altering the collective memory and perception of an organization by essentially creating myths is difficult and requires joint efforts of many stakeholders sharing the same interests to push an agenda.

STEP THREE

Building the Bargepole Persona: Above Reproach and Scrutiny

As the name bargepole suggests, the theory is about creating distances and avoiding any direct involvement by acting out the role of a balanced, wise, and unbiased leader. As such, openness and honesty are a liability that can be used against a bargepole manager.

In order to avoid this liability, the approach is to act superior and stuck up. Avoiding expressions of heartfelt honesty will keep people unsure of where you stand and keep them uncertain. This will prevent any group from categorizing you unfavorably or wanting to keep you at a distance. However, doing so without having people turn against you or ostracizing you as irrelevant is a fine art to master.

Those people capable of nurturing and portraying a seemingly captivating persona by being inaccessible have a great advantage. Some of the most hypnotically entrancing personas of all time include people such as Marilyn Monroe, Adolf Hitler, and Michael Jackson.

It is almost impossible to know, given what they allowed the public to see and to what extent they were naturally themselves, how much of their personas were consciously developed acts. However, by keeping their personalities inaccessible through their lack of interviews or public appearances, they could nurture the public's fascination with them.

Charles de Gaulle wrote about the need to create distance as being vital for a leader: "there can be no prestige without mystery, for familiarity breeds contempt […] In the designs, the demeanor, and the mental operations of a leader there must always be 'something' which others cannot altogether fathom, which puzzles them, stirs them, and rivets their attention…"

There is general wisdom to be drawn from the power of being inaccessible and unpredictable. Below is a detailed outline of options or approaches for how to craft the bargepole persona.

TACTIC 1. REFRAIN FROM DISPLAYING CANDID EMOTIONS

Unpredictability, keeping your cards close to your chest and having an air of mystery to your presence is a good foundation for creating an atmosphere of anticipation and caution around you. This can be used as an advantage to avoid being questioned and confronted by colleagues.

Yet it is important to note that bargepolers are not devoid of emotions because such emotional emptiness would be a disadvantage to them. Instead, they are able to prevent emotion from clouding their behavior and decision-making.

Most perceived problems, conflicts, and even crises are emotional at their core. As such, these issues may not require any decision to be made. Problems can magically subside on their own by deciding not to decide, detracting focus from a problem, and soothing hot heads and frustrations.

An individual who possesses a consistent demeanor, regardless of the situation and information available, is seen as a strong leader. Our nature is to seek out leaders with emotional stability. In times of crises, we instinctively want someone to tell us that everything is going to be okay, even if we are on a sinking lifeboat with only a few minutes left to live.

More often than not, simply not acting in a crisis, is preferable to thinking that reactionary measures can change the outcome. The more likely outcome of over-reacting is implicating yourself in matters you can't explain. Particularly in crises, there can be great advantages to adopting the philosophy of "Don't just do something… Stand there and look important!"

TACTIC 2: RELY ON PERSONALITY AND LIKABILITY

This second alternative is much less common, and it is also less available as an option. Instead of closing yourself off and finding ways to be formal and inaccessible by being less personal and emotional, this alternative embraces the opposite approach. Through a type of reverse psychology of being considered approachable and genuine, you will able to hide behind a cloak of sincerity and emotion.

Politicians are the most obvious example of users of this approach. Former President Bill Clinton is a good example. Although he lied and was exposed for his mendacity, many held that his actions were further proof of personable and genuine demeanor.

These bargepole managers are essentially skilled actors. They engage and operate within their organization as if it were their stage and as if their colleagues were their audience. As will be described later in more detail, bargepole managers tend to display strong tendencies of narcissism along with a sense of entitlement. To them, this justifies insincere relationships so as to take advantage of people.

The best bargepole managers will never reveal anything substantial or significant about their identities or backgrounds that can be verified independently. They may make members in an organization think they have a clear idea about their identities and portray themselves as being sincere and honest, but they will never invite you to their homes. More importantly, they will never introduce you to any of their personal friends who can connect them to a wider social network; this would risk exposure.

An additional strategy is to feign strong loyalty in a very intimate and personal way and serenade egos. By tailoring your 'value proposition' as a bargepoler, you project the idea that you are a valuable point of contact and that it is in the best interest of others to support you. This strategy of faking identities and emotional attachments to people for personal benefit has become an increasingly accepted norm in a career environment where everyone is a salesperson regardless of his or her job description. However, this does not mean that having the talent of being a credible phony is by any means sufficient to becoming a bargepole manager.

TACTIC 3. BUILD A PERSONAL BRAND

The third alternative is a form of master class, a proficiency at being above reproach so as to deflect accountability by means of building a personal brand. This alternative really only applies to the superstars of Bargepoling.

President John F. Kennedy was often able to stand above reproach and criticism. Examples include the Bay of Pigs fiasco or initiating the first large escalation of the Vietnam War. Yet Kennedy's name only gets mentioned in connection with his supposed plans to end the war.

President Ronald Reagan's greatness came from his ability to constantly maintain and uphold the illusion of transparency and authenticity of being a man of the people while simultaneously maintaining a super hero status. But his greatest achievement was that he actually managed to credibly deflect the many atrociously bad initiatives he was behind while simultaneously taking credit for everything good that happened overall. As a result, President Reagan was one of the greatest bargepolers of all time.

During the Iran-Contra affair, President Reagan set the gold standard of Bargepole Management when he let Oliver North take the complete rap and fall in the public spotlight. And even while there was evidence he had been briefed about the details, he explained that he had either not understood or that he may have even been asleep during these meetings. As you can easily appreciate, the use of 'being asleep' as an excuse for not taking responsibility is pure master class! Many great bargepolers have attempted similar excuses since this occurrence, but no one ever got away with it as graciously as President Reagan. The possible exception is when President Clinton avoided giving a straight answer by saying, "It depends on what the definition of is, is."

President Clinton is similar in his incredible and undeniable greatness. Despite his personal flaws, no one is so naïve as to believe the supposed good job or the excuses he claimed concerning interns in the Oval Office. Not only did he get away with such discrepancies, but he ultimately became admired for them. He also received the credit for helping to launch his wife's political career as a convenient side effect.

These great leaders in history are united by their incredible skill at communication, their way of presenting themselves, and their largely average intellect, enabling them to completely overshadow reality. While these leaders are examples of formidable rhetorical skill, their approach was style over substance. This commonality is despite each leader being unmistakably unique and contagious while saying some of the best one-liners in political history.

Bargepoling that is based on building a personal brand is achieved by using personally emotional storytelling. Typical ingredients include a sympathetic face with whom we can easily identify and a story of overcoming great odds with perseverance and great self-sacrifice. In the United States, politicians commonly include a narrative of overcoming personal weaknesses and temptations. There are no lack of examples, from President George W. Bush and alcoholism to Elliot Spitzer and prostitutes.

In both politics and business, the ability to be presentable, together with a marketable persona, is becoming ever more important. It is fair game, and it is unlikely to change. Good things can be accomplished through a personal brand that enables extreme Bargepoling. It's particularly good for propping up stock prices, as is the case with billionaire Richard Branson.

Less positive and obvious comparisons are Bernie Madoff and Kenneth Lay (former CEO of Enron). These men also had amazing life stories as they made something from nothing through sheer will and ingenuity. However, in their cases, the outcomes were less beneficial for their believers who let their claims go unquestioned.

Being populist and charismatic can be a powerful force. Uniting and rallying people to work with improved harmony and thereby avoid infighting can often be an end in and of itself, which should not be overlooked as a function of leadership. But just as populism and charisma can become a powerful force for the positive, they can also be abused as forms of immunity against the public's distrust.

In stark contrast to leaders who have been able to successfully use a bargepole persona as a form of immunity against mistakes and personal transgressions is President Richard Nixon. Of all the U.S. presidents, he probably failed the worst at Bargepoling. It is difficult to fully comprehend how he managed to implicate himself, get impeached, and resign over a largely insignificant burglary. At the same time, he managed to forfeit taking the credit for ending the Vietnam War with Henry Kissinger taking all the glory as the recipient of the Nobel Peace Prize.

It should be noted that wanting to be a high-profile politician or CEO and draw attention to oneself generally goes against the nature of bargepoling. Such positions make it very difficult to evade scrutiny and criticism of leadership or lack thereof. Being in the background and securing a cushy position that is protected and away from the spotlight is more akin to bargepole management theory. However, charismatic and enigmatic leaders offer many lessons for how to build a bargepole persona.

DANGERS AND PITFALLS TO THE BARGEPOLE MANAGER

Delusional Hubris and Tunnel Vision

Experienced bargepolers recognize that one of the largest threats to their success is self-belief in the value and importance of their own charade. Bargepolers must maintain an accurate self-awareness, and this objective is a continuous challenge because it runs counter to projecting an image of superior knowledge. In turn, this image of superior knowledge makes it difficult to solicit honest opinions and feedback.

The temptation to seek support for beliefs and ideas by surrounding yourself with 'yes-men' easily leads to both distorted decision-making and misdirected focus. A common situation is when bizarre details take priority over operational emergencies. Examples include the overzealous control of minor expenditures such as printing paper or 'perfecting' aesthetic details of irrelevant matters with little consequence such as promotional materials or office seating arrangements. The longer a manager surrounds himself with sycophants, the easier it is to unknowingly succumb to such vanities.

The Bargepoler's Dilemma

The process of creating barriers to entry for a market competitor is well-covered in economic theory. These barriers to entry are also a major element for a bargepoler who wishes to protect his or her position from challengers in a hierarchy.

Similarly, benefits can be reaped from a concept known as first-mover advantage, which involves having the good sense and fortune of being first to enter a market, product niche, or company while there is little competition. While first-mover advantage has often been the scenario of many market leaders, market dominance is rarely about merely being first.

Instead, seizing the first-mover advantage is more about laying claim to a sufficient size territory in order to create and leverage the benefits of inequalities that arise and result in an uneven playing field. Many companies that have been able to reach a position of dominance in a market tend to share this trait. Competitors are crowded out through advantages of scale in production and/or distribution. John Rockefeller dominated rail transportation by owning railroads that provided access to distribution. Microsoft holds its position largely because of needs for compatibility. Amazon built a supplier and distribution system of incomparable reach and efficiency.

Despite how commonly seen and understood this principle is in markets, there is rarely much discussion on strategies for corporations to benefit from stifling change and progress to maintain these advantages. Maxims such as 'innovate or die' are far more palatable. While the value of continuous innovation cannot be understated, the inherent difficulties in upholding a consistent level of performance are often, if not completely, overlooked. The term 'status quo' has negative connotations and is often deceptively understood as a euphemism for complacency.

When a bargepole manager has reached a position where they have created inequalities from which they are able to leverage and benefit, their success can become like a disease. Satisfaction can become a state of no satisfaction. Inevitably, nothing fails like success. Given sufficient time, success can have no place left to go with nothing left to prove. This predicament is the most challenging of circumstances and poses many threats. If the status quo of a current position is the best realistic scenario, the ability to bargepole effectively can become severely problematic.

Herein lies the Bargepoler's Dilemma. On one hand, the bargepoler must not underestimate the discipline and hard work required to uphold the status quo of the Bargepole Hierarchy. On the other hand, the bargepoler must not attempt to overreach by taking unnecessary risks; these risks can also destabilize his or her position or operations of the organization.

Even for the best bargepolers, who have mastered accurate awareness, the seduction of overestimating their own abilities is always lurking in the back of their minds. Remember how Coca Cola decided to launch 'New Coke', and the failure it resulted in for both the company and for those employees responsible? There was a status quo which should not have been challenged!

Overcoming the Bargepoler's Dilemma requires the stamina of enthusiasm. As seen in countless Hollywood movies, enthusiasm alone can make up for any number of shortcomings in overcoming incalculable odds. Though these movies are mostly exaggerated, it is nonetheless the case that our capability is directly constrained by our level of enthusiasm. Enthusiasm is the fuel that feeds the fire of resolve and perseverance. Put simply, the secret is to not let boredom seep in. We have an overpowering urge for novelty and for the sense of moving forward if we are to maintain enthusiasm.

This principle is applicable for both the bargepoler as well as the people being bargepoled. Do not forget that the main responsibility of the bargepoler is to uphold the False Meritocracy that holds the entire bargepole structure together. All bargepole techniques are worthless unless an image of decisive leadership, no matter how disingenuous, is being portrayed. Yet it is just as important to provide the motivators of a cause, a carrot, and the idea of a challenge the jimpees will think is worth fighting for.

On the surface, Bargepoling is an automated operation that maximizes the utility of resources by means of interchangeable jimpees; the jimpees are like units in a factory. The model works perfectly - until it doesn't. Despite, or maybe because of, increasing uniformity of jobs in corporations, their competitiveness depends more than ever on the ability to stir up enthusiasm among jimpees. Encapsulated in the efficiency wage theory, people are emotive and if they pick up on that they are being treated unfairly it affects their productivity negatively. This is a principal threat to be aware of when practicing Bargepoling as it can lead to organizational breakdown.

Ultimately, nothing that is human can thrive without enthusiasm. Whether a patron, bargepoler, firewall, or jimpee, all of us are human, and our need for a sense of belonging and purpose, whether fake or real, is non-negotiable.

Bargepole Management

APPENDIX

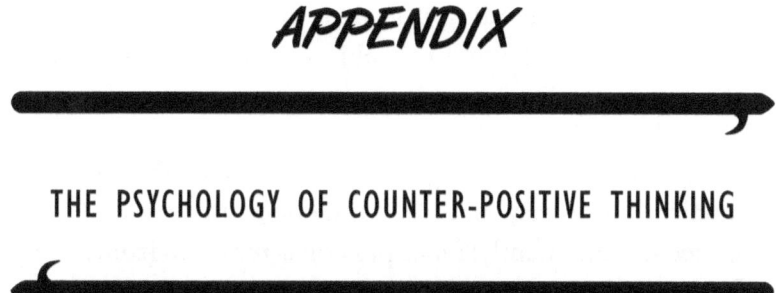

THE PSYCHOLOGY OF COUNTER-POSITIVE THINKING

"Intense feeling too often obscures the truth."
—Harry Truman

Most beliefs and positions are based on the motivation to make us feel good irrespective of reality. Influencing people to disregard facts and logic unwittingly is a powerful weapon for pushing an agenda. Understanding this vulnerability in people is bargepole psychology. The practice of exploiting it is part of bargepole management and where Counter-Positive Thinking comes in. Below is an outline for how to practice it..

STEP ONE:

LET GO OF TRYING TO FIND YOUR PASSION

Passion is not an enabler. Instead, passion is a distraction that can only get you so far. An inconvenient fact about passion is that you probably don't have enough of it anyway, or you are simply unable to channel it productively. Many people can relate to going to bed with the intention of, and sometimes the expectation of, making love all night, yet they find themselves falling asleep after twenty minutes or so of action.

When it comes to succeeding in a corporate career, personal discipline trumps passion every time! Bargepoling is about laying claim to a piece of valuable territory and defending it against intruders who also want that same piece of territory. To fulfill this objective, it makes sense to assume that following your passion is sure to severely misguide you.

So how does passion relate to Bargepole Management? Passion is a liability for a bargepoler. This is easy to understand conceptually but it is extremely difficult to execute consistently! Once passion is removed from the equation, you can easily identify a market where your limited skills and capacity can be presented as valuable and a situation where the competition is weak and difficult to objectively compare.

STEP TWO:

SUPERIOR SELF-AWARENESS

Talented bargepolers accept that they are largely average and not significantly smarter or with a professional skill set remarkably different from most of their colleagues. Critically connected with this is that their colleagues lack this insight and are under the flawed assumption that rewards are connected to their contribution to value creation.

If you belong to the minority that understands that you are not as smart in real life as you are in your fantasies, then you have strong potential to become a successful bargepoler. This statement assumes that you can exploit the weaknesses of your competitors who lack this insight and that those competitors can be misled due to their delusional self-perception.

STEP THREE:

APPLYING THE PSYCHOLOGY OF COUNTER-POSITIVE THINKING

Counter-Positive Psychology is what enables you to gain a competitive edge over colleagues in assessing, distorting, and obscuring information for the purpose of presenting your chosen perspective that becomes the reality of the power patron(s) that secures your bargepole position.

Counter-Positive Psychology is not to be confused with pessimism or having a negative attitude. Instead, Counter-Positive Psychology is about allowing others to be unrealistically optimistic while you stand on the sidelines and exploit them!

Positive Thinking is essentially a practice in underestimating risks and overestimating available resources and is often called optimism, which explains a lot of failures of both organizations and individuals. The contradiction inherent for people that subscribe to ideas of Positive Psychology is that by having an exaggerated faith in their own abilities, underestimating the obstacles and the difficulties, and simply expecting favorable outcomes, they can find motivation to perform better than they would otherwise. If you want your army to enthusiastically charge enemy lines despite abysmal odds, preaching positive thinking to those who are fighting the battles, to those who are taking the losses, and to those who will later let you take credit for victory, is advised. Counter-Positive Psychology is the juxtaposition where a more accurate understanding of causation, as well as an awareness of how positivity distorts the ability of people around you to think rationally, gives an edge to manipulate those with overly simplistic views of reality.

Counter-Positive Psychology goes hand-in-hand with the first step of letting go of your passion and with the second step of exploiting the weaknesses of others who overestimate their prospects and abilities.

Awareness of how people overestimate their abilities makes it easier to manipulate and take advantage of them. Bargepolers want to attract people that are non-questioning of False Meritocracies and the prospects of advancement. These people are most easily exploited by dangling a carrot in front of them and giving positive reinforcement by agreeing with what they are already brainwashing themselves with.

The practice of Counter-Positive Psychology in Bargepole Management is to objectively observe a situation while seeing how others may be misinterpreting the same information available. Thereafter, the skill is to determine how to play these misunderstandings to your advantage.

.

Minimal Input - Maximum Gain

Bargepole Management

Minimal Input - Maximum Gain